OUR

FREEDOM

DOCUMENTS

Compiled by

ROBERT B. WATTS, 33°, G∴C∴

Director of Education

THE SUPREME COUNCIL, 33°

ANCIENT AND ACCEPTED SCOTTISH RITE OF FREEMASONRY
FOR THE SOUTHERN JURISDICTION OF THE UNITED STATES OF AMERICA
(MOTHER SUPREME COUNCIL OF THE WORLD)
1733 16TH STREET N.W., WASHINGTON, D. C. 20009

CONTENTS

PRICE $2.00 PER COPY

Orders should be accompanied by payments and addressed to: The Supreme Council, 33°. 1733 Sixteenth Street N.W., Washington, D. C. 20009.

FOREWORD

In order to form a base for the "Dynamic Freedoms" booklets which will follow, we are presenting first what in effect are the life-giving and freedom-giving documents of our country. No one can begin to understand the great triumph which was achieved in the formation of the government under which we live without knowing and understanding these. For example, how many people have read our Constitution? Yet this can be done in twenty minutes!

In these "Freedom Documents" are to be found a deep belief and faith in God, a recognition of the age-old yearnings of men for liberty and dignity, a set of guarantees for the protection of individual rights against ancient abuses, and the reservation in the people of the ultimate power to amend their form of government by prescribed orderly procedures.

Equally made clear, as in Washington's Farewell Address, is the fact that, "The very idea of the power and the right of the People to establish Government presupposes the duty of every Individual to obey the established Government."

The more important of these "Freedom Documents", including some material not heretofore in our booklets, are presented in this booklet. It is the first of a new series on "Dynamic Freedoms" which will be published by The Supreme Council, 33°.

It is hoped that they may be widely read and distributed.

Sovereign Grand Commander

THE MAYFLOWER COMPACT

November 11, 1620

I N THE NAME OF GOD, AMEN. We whose names are underwritten, the Loyal Subjects of our dread Sovereign Lord King *James,* by the Grace of God, of *Great Britain, France,* and *Ireland,* King, *Defender of the Faith,* &c. Having undertaken, for the Glory of God, and Advancement of the Christian Faith, and Honour of our King and Country, a Voyage to plant the first Colony in the northern Parts of *Virginia;* Do by these Presents solemnly and mutually in the Presence of God, and one another, covenant and combine ourselves together into a civil Body Politick, for our better Ordering and Preservation and Furtherance of the Ends aforesaid; And by Virtue hereof to enact, constitute, and frame such just and equal Laws, Ordinances, Acts, Constitutions, and Officers, from time to time, as shall be thought most meet and convenient for the general Good of the Colony; unto which we promise all due Submission and Obedience. IN WITNESS whereof we have hereunder subscribed our names at *Cape-Cod* the eleventh of *November,* in the year of the Reign of our Sovereign Lord, King *James,* of *England, France,* and *Ireland,* the eighteenth and of *Scotland,* the fifty-fourth, *Anno Domini,* 1620.

(The original list of signers has disappeared. Nathaniel Morton, writing in 1669, listed forty-one signers of the document. Channing, Edward, A History of the United States, 6 vols., 1928, I, chap. 11.)

THE CALL TO ARMS

PATRICK HENRY
1775

MR. PRESIDENT, it is natural to man to indulge in the illusions of hope. We are apt to shut our eyes against a painful truth. Is this the part of wise men, engaged in a great and arduous struggle for liberty? Are we disposed to be of the number of those, who, having eyes, see not, and having ears, hear not, the things which so nearly concern their temporal salvation? For my part, whatever anguish of spirit it may cost, I am willing to know the whole truth; to know the worst, and to provide for it.

I have but one lamp by which my feet are guided; and that is the lamp of experience. I know of no way of judging of the future but by the past. Let us not, I beseech you, sir, deceive ourselves longer. Sir, we have done everything that could be done to avert the storm which is now coming on. We have petitioned; we have remonstrated; we have supplicated; we have prostrated ourselves before the throne, and have implored its interposition to arrest the tyrannical hands of the ministry and Parliament. Our petitions have been slighted; our remonstrances have produced additional violence and insult; our supplications have been disregarded; and we have been spurned, with contempt, from the foot of the throne! In vain, after these things, may we indulge the fond hope of peace and reconciliation. There is no longer any room for hope. If we wish to be free— if we mean to preserve inviolate those inestimable privileges for which we have been so long contending—if we mean not basely to abandon the noble struggle in which we have been so long engaged, and which we have pledged ourselves never to abandon, until the glorious object of our contest shall be obtained—we must fight! I repeat it, sir, we must fight! An appeal to arms and to the God of Hosts is all that is left us!

They tell us, sir, that we are weak—unable to cope with so formidable an adversary. But when shall we be stronger? Will it be the next week, or the next year? Will it be when we are totally disarmed? Shall we acquire the means of effectual resistance by lying supinely on our backs and hugging the delusive phantom of hope, until our enemies shall have bound us hand and foot?

Sir, we are not weak if we make a proper use of those means which the God of nature has placed in our power. Three millions of people armed in the holy cause of liberty, and in such a country as

5

PATRICK HENRY
1736 - 1799

THE CALL TO ARMS

that which we possess, are invincible by any force which our enemy can send against us. Besides, sir, we shall not fight our battles alone. There is a just God who presides over the destines of nations, and who will raise up friends to fight our battles for us. The battle, sir, is not to the strong alone; it is to the vigilant, the active, the brave.

It is in vain, sir, to extenuate the matter. Gentleman may cry "Peace, peace"—But there is no peace. The war is actually begun! Our brethren are already in the field! Why stand we here idle? What is it that gentlemen wish? What would they have? Is life so dear, or peace so sweet, as to be purchased at the price of chains and slavery? Forbid it, Almighty God! I know not what course others may take; but as for me, give me liberty or give me death!

———————

Every tomorrow has two handles. You can take hold of tomorrow with the handle of anxiety or you can take hold of it with the handle of faith.

—Henry Ward Beecher

THE GREATEST BELL IN THE WORLD

The Liberty Bell as it appears today in Independence Hall, Philadelphia, Pa. The circumference around the lip is 12 feet; around the crown, 7 feet 6 inches. From lip to crown measures 3 feet, and the clapper is 3 feet 2 inches long. The metal is 3 inches thick at the lip, and the over-all weight is 2080 pounds.

THE DECLARATION OF INDEPENDENCE

IN CONGRESS, JULY 4, 1776

WHEN in the Course of human events, it becomes necessary for one people to dissolve the political bands which have connected them with another, and to assume among the powers of the earth, the separate and equal station to which the Laws of Nature and of Nature's God entitle them, a decent respect to the opinions of mankind requires that they should declare the causes which impel them to the separation.

We hold these truths to be self-evident, that all men are created equal, that they are endowed by their Creator with certain unalienable Rights, that among these are Life, Liberty and the pursuit of Happiness. That to secure these rights, Governments are instituted among Men, deriving their just powers from the consent of the governed. That whenever any Form of Government becomes destructive of these ends, it is the Right of the People to alter or to abolish it, and to institute new Government, laying its foundation on such principles and organizing its powers in such form, as to them shall seem most likely to effect their Safety and Happiness. Prudence, indeed, will dictate that Governments long established should not be changed for light and transient causes; and accordingly all experience hath shewn that mankind are more disposed to suffer, while evils are sufferable, than to right themselves by abolishing the forms to which they are accustomed. But when a long train of abuses and usurpations, pursuing invariably the same Object evinces a design to reduce them under absolute Despotism, it is their right, it is their duty, to throw off such Government, and to provide new Guards for their future security. Such has been the patient sufferance of these Colonies; and such is now the necessity which constrains them to alter their former Systems of Government. The history of the present King of Great Britain is a history of repeated injuries and usurpations, all having in direct object the establishment of an absolute Tyranny over these States. To prove this, let Facts be submitted to a candid world.

He has refused his Assent to Laws, the most wholesome and necessary for the public good. He has forbidden his Governors to pass Laws of immediate and pressing importance, unless suspended in their operation till his Assent should be obtained; and when so suspended, he has utterly neglected to attend to them.

He has refused to pass other Laws for the accommodation of large districts of people, unless those people would relinquish the right of Representation in the Legislature, a right inestimable to them and formidable to tyrants only.

He has called together legislative bodies at places unusual, uncomfortable, and distant from the depository of their public Records, for the sole purpose of fatiguing them into compliance with his measures.

He has dissolved Representative Houses repeatedly, for opposing with manly firmness his invasions on the rights of the people.

He has refused for a long time, after such dissolutions, to cause others to be elected; whereby the Legislative powers, incapable of Annihilation, have returned to the People at large for their exercise; the State remaining in the meantime exposed to all the dangers of invasion from without, and convulsions within.

He has endeavored to prevent the population of these States; for that purpose obstructing the Laws of Naturalization of Foreigners; refusing to pass others to encourage their migrations hither, and raising the conditions of new Appropriations of Lands.

He has obstructed the Administration of Justice, by refusing his Assent to Laws for establishing Judiciary Powers.

He has made Judges dependent on his Will alone, for the tenure of their offices, and the amount and payment of their salaries.

He has erected a multitude of New Offices, and sent hither swarms of Officers to harass our people, and eat out their substance.

He has kept among us, in times of peace, Standing Armies without the Consent of our legislatures.

He has affected to render the Military independent of and superior to the Civil power.

He has combined with others to subject us to a jurisdiction foreign to our constitution, and unacknowledged by our laws; giving his Assent to their Acts of pretended Legislation: For quartering large bodies of armed troops among us: For protecting them, by a mock Trial, from punishment for any Murders which they should commit on the Inhabitants of these States: For cutting off our Trade with all parts of the world: For imposing Taxes on us without our

Consent: For depriving us in many cases, of the benefits of Trial by Jury: For transporting us beyond Seas to be tried for pretended offences: For abolishing the free System of English Laws in a neighbouring Province, establishing therein an Arbitrary government, and enlarging its Boundaries so as to render it at once an example and fit instrument for introducing the same absolute rule into these Colonies: For taking away our Charters, abolishing our most valuable Laws, and altering fundamentally the Forms of our Governments: For suspending our own Legislatures, and declaring themselves invested with power to legislate for us in all cases whatsoever.

He has abdicated Government here, by declaring us out of his Protection and waging War against us.

He has plundered our seas, ravaged our Coasts, burnt our towns, and destroyed the lives of our people.

He is at this time transporting large Armies of foreign Mercenaries to complete the works of death, desolation and tyranny, already begun with circumstances of Cruelty & perfidy scarcely paralleled in the most barbarous ages, and totally unworthy the Head of a civilized nation.

He has constrained our fellow Citizens taken Captive on the high Seas to bear Arms against their Country, to become the executioners of their friends and Brethren, or to fall themselves by their Hands.

He has excited domestic insurrections amongst us, and has endeavored to bring on the inhabitants of our frontiers, the merciless Indian Savages, whose known rule of warfare, is an undistinguished destruction of all ages, sexes and conditions.

In every stage of these Oppressions We have Petitioned for Redress in the most humble terms: Our repeated Petitions have been answered only by repeated injury. A Prince, whose character is thus marked by every act which may define a Tyrant, is unfit to be the ruler of a free people. Nor have We been wanting in attentions to our British brethren. We have warned them from time to time of attempts by their legislature to extend an unwarrantable jurisdiction over us. We have reminded them of the circumstances of our emigration and settlement here. We have appealed to their native justice and magnanimity, and we have conjured them by the ties of our common kindred to disavow these usurpations, which would inevitably interrupt our connections and correspondence. They too have been deaf to the voice of justice and of consanguinity. We must, therefore, acquiesce in the necessity, which denounces our Separation, and hold them, as we hold the rest of mankind, Enemies in War, in Peace, Friends.

WE THEREFORE, the Representatives of the UNITED STATES OF AMERICA, in General Congress, Assembled, appealing to the Supreme Judge of the world for the rectitude of our intentions, do, in the Name, and by Authority of the Good People of these Colonies, solemnly publish and declare, That these United Colonies are, and of Right ought to be FREE AND INDEPENDENT STATES; that they are Absolved from all Allegiance to the British Crown, and that all political connection between them and the State of Great Britain, is and ought to be totally dissolved; and that as Free and Independent States, they have full Power to levy War, conclude Peace, contract Alliances, establish Commerce, and to do all other Acts and Things which Independent States may of right do. And for the support of this Declaration, with a firm reliance on the protection of Divine Providence, we mutually pledge to each other our Lives, our Fortunes and our sacred Honor.

THOMAS JEFFERSON
1743 - 1826

Author of the Declaration of Independence

The Shrine Containing the
Declaration of Independence
and the
Constitution of the United States
of America.

THE CONSTITUTION
OF THE
UNITED STATES OF AMERICA

PREAMBLE

WE THE PEOPLE of the United States, in Order to form a more perfect Union, establish Justice, insure domestic Tranquility, provide for the common defense, promote the general Welfare, and secure the Blessings of Liberty to ourselves and our Posterity, do ordain and establish this Constitution for the United States of America.

ARTICLE I

SECTION 1

Legislative powers vested in Congress

All legislative Powers herein granted shall be vested in a Congress of the United States, which shall consist of a Senate and House of Representatives.

SECTION 2

Composition of the House of Representatives

1. The House of Representatives shall be composed of Members chosen every second Year by the People of the several States, and the Electors in each State shall have the Qualifications requisite for Electors of the most numerous Branch of the State Legislature.

Qualification of Representatives

2. No Person shall be a Representative who shall not have attained to the Age of twenty-five Years, and been seven Years a Citizen of the United States, and who shall not, when elected, be an Inhabitant of that State in which he shall be chosen.

Apportionment of Representatives and direct taxes—census*

3. [Representatives and direct Taxes shall be apportioned among the several States which may be included within this Union, according to their respective Numbers, which shall be determined by adding to the whole Number of free Persons, including those bound to Service for

---

* *The clause included in brackets is amended by the 14th Amendment, Section 2.*

15

a Term of Years, and excluding Indians not taxed, three fifths of all other Persons.] The actual Enumeration shall be made within three Years after the first Meeting of the Congress of the United States, and within every subsequent Term of ten Years, in such Manner as they shall by Law direct. The Number of Representatives shall not exceed one for every thirty Thousand, but each State shall have at Least one Representative; and until such enumeration shall be made, the State of New Hampshire shall be entitled to chuse three, Massachusetts eight, Rhode Island and Providence Plantations one, Connecticut five, New York six, New Jersey four, Pennsylvania eight, Delaware one, Maryland six, Virginia ten, North Carolina five, South Carolina five, and Georgia three.

Filling of vacancies in representation

4. When vacancies happen in the Representation from any State, the Executive Authority thereof shall issue Writs of Election to fill such Vacancies.

Selection of officers; power of impeachment

5. The House of Representatives shall chuse their Speaker and other Officers; and shall have the sole Power of Impeachment.

The Senate
SECTION 3†

[1. The Senate of the United States shall be composed of two Senators from each State, chosen by the Legislature thereof, for six Years; and each Senator shall have one Vote.]

Classification of Senators; filling of vacancies

2. Immediately after they shall be assembled in Consequence of the first Election, they shall be divided as equally as may be into three Classes. The Seats of the Senators of the first Class shall be vacated at the Expiration of the second Year, of the second Class at the Expiration of the fourth Year, and of the third Class at the Expiration of the sixth Year, so that one-third may be chosen every second Year; and if Vacancies happen by Resignation, or otherwise, during the Recess of the Legislature of any State, the Executive thereof may make temporary Appointments [until the next Meeting of the Legislature, which shall then fill such Vacancies].

---

† *The 1st paragraph of this section and as much of the 2nd paragraph as relates to filling vacancies are amended by the 17th Amendment.*

Qualification of Senators

3. No Person shall be a Senator who shall not have attained the Age of thirty Years, and been nine Years a Citizen of the United States, and who shall not, when elected, be an Inhabitant of that State for which he shall be chosen.

Vice President to be President of Senate

4. The Vice President of the United States shall be President of the Senate, but shall have no Vote, unless they be equally divided.

Selection of Senate officers; President pro tempore

5. The Senate shall chuse their other Officers, and also a President pro tempore, in the Absence of the Vice President, or when he shall exercise the Office of President of the United States.

Senate to try impeachments

6. The Senate shall have the sole Power to try all Impeachments. When sitting for that Purpose, they shall be on Oath or Affirmation. When the President of the United States is tried, the Chief Justice shall preside: And no Person shall be convicted without the Concurrence of two thirds of the Members present.

Judgment in cases of impeachment

7. Judgment in Cases of Impeachment shall not extend further than to removal from Office, and disqualification to hold and enjoy any Office of honor, Trust or Profit under the United States: but the Party convicted shall nevertheless be liable and subject to Indictment, Trial, Judgment and Punishment, according to Law.

SECTION 4

Control of congressional elections

1. The Times, Places and Manner of holding Elections for Senators and Representatives, shall be prescribed in each State by the Legislature thereof; but the Congress may at any time by Law make or alter such Regulations, except as to the Places of chusing Senators.

Time for assembling of Congress†

2. The Congress shall assemble at least once in every Year, and such Meeting shall be on the first Monday in December, unless they shall by Law appoint a different Day.

† *Amended by the 20th Amendment, Section 2.*

Section 5

Each house to be the judge of the election and qualifications of its members; regulations as to quorum

1. Each House shall be the Judge of the Elections, Returns and Qualifications of its own Members, and a Majority of each shall constitute a Quorum to do Business; but a smaller Number may adjourn from day to day, and may be authorized to compel the Attendance of absent Members, in such Manner, and under such Penalties as each House may provide.

Each house to determine its own rules

2. Each House may determine the Rules of its Proceedings, punish its Members for disorderly Behaviour, and, with the Concurrence of two thirds, expel a Member.

Journals and yeas and nays

3. Each House shall keep a Journal of its Proceedings, and from time to time publish the same, excepting such Parts as may in their Judgment require Secrecy; and the Yeas and Nays of the Members of either House on any question shall, at the Desire of one fifth of those Present, be entered on the Journal.

Adjournment

4. Neither House, during the Session of Congress shall, without the Consent of the other, adjourn for more than three days, nor to any other Place than that in which the two Houses shall be sitting.

Section 6

Compensation and privileges of Members of Congress

1. The Senators and Representatives shall receive a Compensation for their Services, to be ascertained by Law, and paid out of the Treasury of the United States. They shall in all Cases, except Treason, Felony and Breach of the Peace, be privileged from Arrest during their Attendance at the Session of their respective Houses, and in going to and returning from the same; and for any Speech or Debate in either House, they shall not be questioned in any other Place.

Incompatable offices; exclusions

2. No Senator or Representative shall, during the Time for which he was elected, be appointed to any civil Office under the Authority of

the United States, which shall have been created, or the Emoluments whereof shall have been encreased during such time; and no Person holding any Office under the United States, shall be a Member of either House during his Continuance of Office.

Revenue bills to originate in House

1. All Bills for raising Revenue shall originate in the House of Representatives; but the Senate may propose or concur with Amendments as on other Bills.

Manner of passing bills; veto power of President

2. Every Bill which shall have passed the House of Representatives and the Senate, shall, before it becomes a Law, be presented to the President of the United States; If he approve he shall sign it, but if not he shall return it, with his Objections to that House in which it shall have originated, who shall enter the Objections at large on their Journal, and proceed to reconsider it. If after such Reconsideration two thirds of that House shall agree to pass the Bill, it shall be sent, together with the Objections, to the other House, by which it shall likewise be reconsidered, and if approved by two thirds of that House, it shall become a Law. But in all such Cases the Votes of both Houses shall be determined by Yeas and Nays, and the Names of the Persons voting for and against the Bill shall be entered on the Journal of each House respectively. If any Bill shall not be returned by the President within ten Days (Sundays excepted) after it shall have been presented to him, the Same shall be a Law, in like Manner as if he had signed it, unless the Congress by their Adjournment prevents its Return, in which Case it shall not be a Law.

Concurrent orders or resolutions, to be passed by President

3. Every Order, Resolution, or Vote to which the Concurrence of the Senate and House of Representatives may be necessary (except on a question of Adjournment) shall be presented to the President of the United States; and before the Same shall take Effect, shall be approved by him, or being disapproved by him, shall be repassed by two thirds of the Senate and House of Representatives, according to the Rules and Limitations prescribed in the Case of a Bill.

THE CONSTITUTION OF THE UNITED STATES

SECTION 8

General powers of Congress

The Congress shall have Power.—1. To lay and collect Taxes, Duties, Imposts and Excises, to pay the Debts and provide for the common Defense and general Welfare of the United States; but all Duties, Imposts and Excises shall be uniform throughout the United States;

Borrowing of money

2. To borrow Money on the credit of the United States;

Regulation of commerce

3. To regulate Commerce with foreign Nations, and among the several States, and with the Indian Tribes;

Naturalization and bankruptcy

4. To establish an uniform Rule of Naturalization, and uniform Laws on the subject of Bankruptcies throughout the United States;

Money, weights and measures

5. To coin Money, regulate the Value thereof, and of foreign Coin, and fix the Standard of Weights and Measures;

Counterfeiting

6. To provide for the Punishment of counterfeiting the Securities and current Coin of the United States;

Post offices

7. To establish Post Offices and post Roads;

Patents and copyrights

8. To promote the Progress of Science and useful Arts, by securing for limited Times to Authors and Inventors the exclusive Right to their respective Writings and Discoveries;

Inferior courts

9. To constitute Tribunals inferior to the supreme Court;

Piracies and felonies

10. To define and punish Piracies and Felonies committed on the high Seas, and Offences against the Law of Nations;

War; marque and reprisal

11. To declare War, grant Letters of Marque and Reprisal, and make Rules concerning Captures on Land and Water;

Armies

12. To raise and support Armies, but no Appropriation of Money to that Use shall be for a longer Term than two Years;

Navy

13. To provide and maintain a Navy;

Land and naval forces

14. To make Rules for the Government and Regulation of the land and naval Forces;

Calling out militia

15. To provide for calling forth the Militia to execute the Laws of the Union, suppress Insurrections and repel Invasions;

Organizing, arming and disciplining militia

16. To provide for organizing, arming, and disciplining, the Militia, and for governing such Part of them as may be employed in the Service of the United States, reserving to the States respectively, the Appointment of the Officers, and the Authority of training the Militia according to the discipline prescribed by Congress;

Exclusive legislation over District of Columbia

17. To exercise exclusive Legislation in all Cases whatsoever, over such District (not exceeding ten Miles square) as may, by Cession of particular States, and the Acceptance of Congress, become the Seat of the Government of the United States, and to exercise like Authority over all Places purchased by the Consent of the Legislature of the State in which the Same shall be, for the Erection of Forts, Magazines, Arsenals, dock-Yards, and other needful Buildings;—And

To enact laws necessary to enforce Constitution

18. To make all Laws which shall be necessary and proper for carrying into Execution the foregoing Powers, and all other Powers vested by this Constitution in the Government of the United States, or in any Department or Officer thereof.

THE CONSTITUTION OF THE UNITED STATES

SECTION 9

Migration or importation of certain persons not to be prohibited before 1808

1. The Migration or Importation of such Persons as any of the States now existing shall think proper to admit, shall not be prohibited by the Congress prior to the Year one thousand eight hundred and eight, but a Tax or duty may be imposed on such Importation, not exceeding ten dollars for each Person.

Writ of habeas corpus not to be suspended; exception

2. The Privilege of the Writ of Habeas Corpus shall not be suspended, unless when in Cases of Rebellion or Invasion the public Safety may require it.

Bills of attainder and ex post facto laws prohibited

3. No Bill of Attainder or ex post facto Law shall be passed.

Capitation and other direct taxes

4. No Capitation, or other direct, Tax shall be laid, unless in Proportion to the Census or Enumeration herein before directed to be taken.*

Exports not to be taxed

5. No Tax or Duty shall be laid on Articles exported from any State.

No preference to be given to ports of any State; interstate shipping

6. No Preference shall be given by any Regulation of Commerce or Revenue to the Ports of one State over those of another: nor shall Vessels bound to, or from, one State, be obliged to enter, clear, or pay Duties in another.

Money, how drawn from treasury; financial statements to be published

7. No Money shall be drawn from the Treasury, but in Consequence of Appropriations made by law; and a regular Statement and Account of the Receipts and Expenditures of all public Money shall be published from time to time.

---

* See the 16th Amendment.

Titles of nobility not to be granted; acceptance by government officers of favors from foreign powers

8. No Title of Nobility shall be granted by the United States: And no Person holding any Office of Profit or Trust under them, shall, without the Consent of the Congress, accept of any present, Emolument, Office, or Title, of any kind whatever, from any King, Prince, or foreign State.

SECTION 10

Limitations of the powers of the several States

1. No State shall enter into any Treaty, Alliance, or Confederation; grant Letters of Marque and Reprisal; coin Money; emit Bills of Credit; make any Thing but gold and silver Coin a Tender in Payment of Debts; pass any Bill of Attainder, ex post facto Law, or Law impairing the Obligation of Contracts, or grant any Title of Nobility.

State imposts and duties

2. No State shall, without the Consent of the Congress, lay any Imposts or Duties on Imports or Exports, except what may be absolutely necessary for executing its inspection Laws: and the net Produce of all Duties and Imposts, laid by any State on Imports or Exports, shall be for the Use of the Treasury of the United States; and all such Laws shall be subject to the Revision and Control of the Congress.

Further restrictions on powers of States

3. No State shall, without the Consent of Congress, lay any Duty of Tonnage, keep Troops, or Ships of War in time of Peace, enter into any Agreement or Compact with another State, or with a foreign Power, or engage in War, unless actually invaded, or in such imminent Danger as will not admit of delay.

ARTICLE II

SECTION 1

The President; the executive power

1. The executive Power shall be vested in a President of the United States of America. He shall hold his Office during the Term of four Years, and, together with the Vice President, chosen for the same Term, be elected, as follows

THE CONSTITUTION OF THE UNITED STATES

Appointment and qualifications of presidential electors

2. Each State shall appoint, in such Manner as the Legislature thereof may direct, a Number of Electors, equal to the whole Number of Senators and Representatives to which the State may be entitled in the Congress: but no Senator or Representative, or Person holding an Office of Trust or Profit under the United States, shall be appointed an Elector.

Original method of electing the President and Vice President *

[The Electors shall meet in their respective States, and vote by Ballot for two Persons, of whom one at least shall not be an Inhabitant of the same State with themselves. And they shall make a List of all the Persons voted for, and of the Number of Votes for each; which List they shall sign and certify, and transmit sealed to the Seat of the Government of the United States, directed to the President of the Senate. The President of the Senate shall, in the Presence of the Senate and House of Representatives, open all the Certificates, and the Votes shall then be counted. The Person having the greatest Number of Votes shall be the President, if such Number be a Majority of the whole Number of Electors appointed; and if there be more than one who have such Majority, and have an equal Number of Votes, then the House of Representatives shall immediately chuse by Ballot one of them for President; and if no Person have a Majority, then from the five highest on the List the said House shall in like Manner chuse the President. But in chusing the President, the Votes shall be taken by States, the Representation from each State having one Vote; A quorum for this Purpose shall consist of a Member or Members from two thirds of the States and a Majority of all the States shall be necessary to a Choice. In every Case, after the Choice of the President, the Person having the greatest Number of Votes of the Electors shall be the Vice President. But if there should remain two or more who have equal Votes, the Senate should chuse from them by Ballot the Vice President.]

Congress may determine time of choosing electors and day for casting their votes

3. The Congress may determine the Time of chusing the Electors, and the Day on which they shall give their Votes; which Day shall be the same throughout the United States.

---

* This clause has been superseded by the 12th Amendment.

24

THE CONSTITUTION OF THE UNITED STATES

Qualifications for the office of President †

4. No Person except a natural born Citizen, or a Citizen of the United States, at the time of the Adoption of this Constitution, shall be eligible to the Office of President; neither shall any Person be eligible to that Office who shall not have attained to the Age of thirty five Years, and been fourteen Years a Resident within the United States.

Filling vacancy in the office of President ‡

5. In Case of the Removal of the President from Office, or of his death, Resignation, or Inability to discharge the Powers and Duties of the said Office, the Same shall devolve on the Vice President, and the Congress may by Law provide for the Case of Removal, Death, Resignation or Inability, both of the President and Vice President, declaring what Officer shall then act as President, and such Officer shall act accordingly, until the Disability be removed, or a President shall be elected.

Compensation of the President

6. The President shall, at stated Times, receive for his Services, a Compensation, which shall neither be encreased nor diminished during the Period for which he shall have been elected, and he shall not receive within that Period any other Emolument from the United States, or any of them.

Oath to be taken by the President

7. Before he enter on the Execution of his Office, he shall take the following Oath or Affirmation:—"I do solemnly swear (or affirm) that I will faithfully execute the Office of President of the United States, and will to the best of my Ability, preserve, protect and defend the Constitution of the United States."

SECTION 2

The President to be commander in chief of army and navy and head of executive departments; may grant reprieves and pardons

1. The President shall be Commander in Chief of the Army and Navy of the United States, and of the Militia of the several States, when

---

† *For qualifications of the Vice President, see 12th Amendment.*
‡ *Amended by the 20th Amendment, Sections 3 and 4.*

called into the actual Service of the United States; he may require the Opinion, in writing, of the principal Officer in each of the executive Departments, upon any Subject relating to the Duties of their respective Offices, and he shall have Power to grant Reprieves and Pardons for Offences against the United States, except in Cases of Impeachment.

President may, with concurrence of Senate, make treaties, appoint ambassadors, etc.; appointment of inferior officers, authority of Congress over

2. He shall have Power, by and with the Advice and Consent of the Senate, to make Treaties, provided two thirds of the Senators present concur; and he shall nominate, and by and with the Advice and Consent of the Senate, shall appoint Ambassadors, other public Ministers and Consuls, Judges of the supreme Court, and all other Officers of the United States, whose Appointments are not herein otherwise provided for, and which shall be established by Law: but the Congress may by Law vest the Appointment of such inferior Officers, as they think proper, in the President alone, in the Courts of Law, or in the Heads of Departments.

President may fill vacancies in office during recess of Senate

3. The President shall have Power to fill up all Vacancies that may happen during the Recess of the Senate, by granting Commissions which shall expire at the End of their next Session.

SECTION 3

President to give advice to Congress; may convene or adjourn it on certain occasions; to receive ambassadors, etc.; have laws executed and commission all officers

He shall from time to time give to the Congress Information of the State of the Union, and recommend to their Consideration such Measures as he shall judge necessary and expedient; he may, on extraordinary Occasions, convene both Houses or either of them, and in Case of Disagreement between them, with Respect to the Time of Adjournment, he may adjourn them to such Time as he shall think proper; he shall receive Ambassadors and other public Ministers; he shall take Care that the Laws be faithfully executed, and shall Commission all the Officers of the United States.

THE CONSTITUTION OF THE UNITED STATES

SECTION 4

All civil officers removable by impeachment

1. The President, Vice President and all civil Officers of the United States, shall be removed from Office on Impeachment for, and Conviction of, Treason, Bribery, or other high Crimes and Misdemeanors.

ARTICLE III

SECTION 1

Judicial powers; how vested; term of office and compensation of judges

The judicial Power of the United States, shall be vested in one supreme Court, and in such inferior Courts as the Congress may from time to time ordain and establish. The Judges, both of the supreme and inferior Courts, shall hold their Offices during good Behaviour, and shall, at stated Times, receive for their Services, a Compensation, which shall not be diminished during their Continuance in Office.

SECTION 2

Jurisdiction of Federal courts*

1. The judicial Power shall extend to all Cases, in Law and Equity, arising under this Constitution, the Laws of the United States, and Treaties made, or which shall be made, under their Authority;—to all Cases affecting Ambassadors, other public Ministers and Consuls;—to all Cases of Admirality and maritime Jurisdiction;—to Controversies to which the United States shall be a Party;—to Controversies between two or more States;—between a State and Citizens of another State;—between Citizens of different States,—between Citizens of the same State claiming Lands under Grants of different States, and between a State, or the Citizens thereof, and foreign States, Citizens or Subjects.

Original and appellate jurisdiction of Supreme Court

2. In all Cases affecting Ambassadors, other public Ministers and Consuls, and those in which a State shall be Party, the supreme Court shall have original Jurisdiction. In all the other Cases before

---

* *This section is abridged by the 11th Amendment.*

THE CONSTITUTION OF THE UNITED STATES

mentioned, the supreme Court shall have appellate Jurisdiction, both as to Law and Fact, with such Exceptions, and under such Regulations as the Congress shall make.

Trial of all crimes, except impeachment, to be by jury

3. The Trial of all Crimes, except in Cases of Impeachment, shall be by Jury; and such Trial shall be held in the State where the said Crimes shall have been committed, but when not committed within any State, the Trial shall be at such Place or Places as the Congress may by Law have directed.

SECTION 3

Treason defined; conviction of

1. Treason against the United States, shall consist only in levying War against them, or in adhering to their Enemies, giving them Aid and Comfort. No Person shall be convicted of Treason unless on the Testimony of two Witnesses to the same overt Act; or on Confession in open Court.

Congress to declare punishment for treason; proviso

2. The Congress shall have Power to declare the Punishment of Treason, but no Attainder of Treason shall work Corruption of Blood, or Forfeiture except during the Life of the Person attained.

ARTICLE IV

SECTION 1

Each State to give full faith and credit to the public acts and records of other States

Full Faith and Credit shall be given in each State to the public Acts, Records, and judicial Proceedings of every other State. And the Congress may by general Laws prescribe the Manner in which such Acts, Records and Proceedings shall be proved, and the Effect thereof.

SECTION 2

Privileges of citizens

1. The Citizens of each State shall be entitled to all Privileges and Immunities of Citizens in the several States.

28

THE CONSTITUTION OF THE UNITED STATES

Extradition between the several States

2. A Person charged in any State with Treason, Felony, or other Crime, who shall flee from Justice, and be found in another State, shall on Demand of the executive Authority of the State from which he fled, be delivered up, to be removed to the State having Jurisdiction of the Crime.

Persons held to labor or service in one State, fleeing to another, to be returned *

3. No Person held to Service or Labour in one State, under the Laws thereof, escaping into another, shall, in Consequence of any Law or Regulation therein, be discharged from such Service or Labour, but shall be delivered up on Claim of the Party to whom such Service or Labour may be due.

SECTION 3

New States

1. New States may be admitted by the Congress into this Union; but no new State shall be formed or erected within the Jurisdiction of any other State; nor any State be formed by the Junction of two or more States, or Parts of States, without the Consent of the Legislatures of the States concerned as well as of the Congress.

Regulations concerning territory

2. The Congress shall have Power to dispose of and make all needful Rules and Regulations respecting the Territory or other Property belonging to the United States; and nothing in this Constitution shall be so construed as to Prejudice any Claims of the United States, or of any particular State.

SECTION 4

Republican form of government and protection guaranteed the several States

The United States shall guarantee to every State in this Union a Republican Form of Government, and shall protect each of them against Invasion; and on Application of the Legislature, or of the Executive (when the Legislature cannot be convened) against domestic Violence.

---

* See the 13th Amendment.

29

THE CONSTITUTION OF THE UNITED STATES

ARTICLE V

Ways in which the Constitution can be amended

The Congress, whenever two thirds of both Houses shall deem it necessary, shall propose Amendments to this Constitution, or, on the Application of the Legislatures of two thirds of the several States, shall call a Convention for proposing Amendments, which, in either Case, shall be valid to all Intents and Purposes, as Part of this Constitution, when ratified by the Legislatures of three fourths of the several States, or by Conventions in three fourths thereof, as the one or the other Mode of Ratification may be proposed by the Congress; Provided that no Amendment which may be made prior to the Year One thousand eight hundred and eight shall in any Manner affect the first and fourth Clauses in the Ninth Section of the first Article; and that no State, without its Consent, shall be deprived of its equal Suffrage in the Senate.

ARTICLE VI

Debts contracted under the confederation secured

1. All Debts contracted and Engagements entered into, before the Adoption of this Constitution, shall be as valid against the United States under this Constitution, as under the Confederation.

Concerning this immortal instrument of government, James Bryce, Viscount of Dechmont, has said:

The Constitution of the United States, including the amendments, may be read aloud in twenty-three minutes. It is about half as long as Saint Paul's Epistle to the Corinthians and one-fourth as long as the Irish Land Act of 1881. History knows few instruments which in so few words lay down equally momentous rules on a vast range of matters of the highest importance and complexity.

30

THE PRESIDENTS
OF THE UNITED STATES
OF AMERICA

Portraits of Presidents reproduced by permission of and copyright by Brown & Bigelow, a Division of Standard Packaging Corporation, St. Paul, Minn.

GEORGE WASHINGTON
1st President 1789-1797

JOHN ADAMS
2nd President 1797-1801

THOMAS JEFFERSON
3rd President 1801-1809

JAMES MADISON
4th President 1809-1817

JAMES MONROE
5th President 1817-1825

JOHN QUINCY ADAMS
6th President 1825-1829

ANDREW JACKSON
7th President 1829-1837

MARTIN VAN BUREN
8th President 1837-1841

WM. HENRY HARRISON
9th President 1841

JOHN TYLER
10th President 1841-1845

JAMES KNOX POLK
11th President 1845-1849

ZACHARY TAYLOR
12th President 1849-1850

MILLARD FILLMORE
13th President 1850-1853

FRANKLIN PIERCE
14th President 1853-1857

JAMES BUCHANAN
15th President 1857-1861

ABRAHAM LINCOLN
16th President 1861-1865

ANDREW JOHNSON
17th President 1865-1869

ULYSSES S. GRANT
18th President 1869-1877

RUTHERFORD B. HAYES
19th President 1877-1881

JAMES A. GARFIELD
20th President 1881

CHESTER A. ARTHUR
21st President 1881-1885

GROVER CLEVELAND
22nd President 1885-1889
24th President 1893-1897

BENJAMIN HARRISON
23rd President 1889-1893

WILLIAM McKINLEY
25th President 1897-1901

THEODORE ROOSEVELT
26th President 1901-1909

WM. HOWARD TAFT
27th President 1909-1913

WOODROW WILSON
28th President 1913-1921

WARREN G. HARDING
29th President 1921-1923

CALVIN COOLIDGE
30th President 1923-1929

HERBERT HOOVER
31st President 1929-1933

FRANKLIN ROOSEVELT
32nd President 1933-1945

HARRY S. TRUMAN
33rd President 1945-1953

DWIGHT D. EISENHOWER
34th President 1953-1961

JOHN F. KENNEDY
35th President 1961-1963

LYNDON B. JOHNSON
36th President 1963-1969

RICHARD M. NIXON
37th President 1969-

34

THE CONSTITUTION OF THE UNITED STATES

Constitution, laws and treaties of the United States to be supreme

2. This Constitution, and the Laws of the United States which shall be made in Pursuance thereof; and all Treaties made, or which shall be made, under the Authority of the United States, shall be the supreme Law of the Land; and the Judges in every State shall be bound thereby, any Thing in the Constitution or Laws of any State to the Contrary notwithstanding.

Who shall take constitutional oath; no religious test as to official qualification

3. The Senators and Representatives before mentioned, and the Members of the several State Legislatures, and all executive and judicial Officers, both of the United States and of the several States, shall be bound by Oath or Affirmation, to support this Constitution; but no religious Test shall ever be required as a Qualification to any Office or public Trust under the United States.

ARTICLE VII

Constitution to be considered adopted when ratified by nine States

The Ratification of the Conventions of nine States shall be sufficient for the Establishment of this Constitution between the States so ratifying the Same.

AMENDMENTS TO THE CONSTITUTION OF THE UNITED STATES

Amendments I to X inclusive are popularly known as the
BILL OF RIGHTS.

ARTICLE I

Freedom of religion, speech, of the press, and right of petition

Congress shall make no law respecting an establishment of religion, or prohibiting the free exercise thereof; or abridging the freedom of speech, or of the press; or the right of the people peaceably to assemble, and to petition the Government for a redress of grievances.

ARTICLE II

Right of people to bear arms not to be infringed

A well regulated Militia, being necessary to the security of a free State, the right of the people to keep and bear Arms, shall not be infringed.

ARTICLE III

Quartering of troops

No Soldier shall, in time of peace be quartered in any house, without the consent of the Owner, nor in time of war, but in a manner to be prescribed by law.

ARTICLE IV

Persons and houses to be secure from unreasonable searches and seizures

The right of the people to be secure in their persons, houses, papers, and effects, against unreasonable searches and seizures, shall not be violated, and no Warrants shall issue, but upon probable cause, supported by Oath or affirmation, and particularly describing the place to be searched, and the persons or things to be seized.

ARTICLE V

Trials for crimes; just compensation for private property taken for public use

No person shall be held to answer for a capital, or otherwise infamous crime, unless on a presentment or indictment of a Grand Jury, except in cases arising in the land or naval forces, or in the Militia, when in actual service in time of War or public danger; nor shall any person be subject for the same offence to be twice put in jeopardy of life or limb, nor shall be compelled in any criminal case to be a witness against himself, nor be deprived of life, liberty, or property, without due process of law; nor shall private property be taken for public use, without just compensation.

THE CONSTITUTION OF THE UNITED STATES

ARTICLE VI

Civil rights in trials for crimes enumerated

In all criminal prosecutions, the accused shall enjoy the right to a speedy and public trial, by an impartial jury of the State and district wherein the crime shall have been committed, which district shall have been previously ascertained by law, and to be informed of the nature and cause of the accusation; to be confronted with the witnesses against him; to have compulsory process for obtaining witnesses in his favor, and to have the Assistance of Counsel for his defense.

ARTICLE VII

Civil rights in civil suits

In Suits at common law, where the value in controversy shall exceed twenty dollars, the right of trial by jury shall be preserved, and no fact tried by a jury, shall be otherwise re-examined in any Court of the United States, than according to the rules of the common law.

ARTICLE VIII

Excessive bail, fines and punishments prohibited

Excessive bail shall not be required, nor excessive fines imposed, nor cruel and unusual punishments inflicted.

ARTICLE IX

Reserved rights of people

The enumeration in the Constitution, of certain rights, shall not be construed to deny or disparage others retained by the people.

ARTICLE X

Powers not delegated, reserved to states and people respectively

The powers not delegated to the United States by the Constitution, nor prohibited by it to the States, are reserved to the States respectively, or to the people.

THE CONSTITUTION OF THE UNITED STATES
ARTICLE XI
Judicial power of United States not to extend to suits against a State

The Judicial power of the United States shall not be construed to extend to any suit in law or equity, commenced or prosecuted against one of the United States by Citizens of another State, or by Citizens or Subjects of any Foreign State.

ARTICLE XII
Present mode of electing President and Vice-President by electors *

The Electors shall meet in their respective states and vote by ballot for President and Vice-President, one of whom, at least, shall not be an inhabitant of the same state with themselves; they shall name in their ballots the person voted for as President, and in distinct ballots the person voted for as Vice-President, and they shall make distinct lists of all persons voted for as President, and of all persons voted for as Vice-President, and of the number of votes for each, which lists they shall sign and certify, and transmit sealed to the seat of the government of the United States, directed to the President of the Senate;—The President of the Senate shall, in the presence of the Senate and House of Representatives, open all the certificates and the votes shall then be counted;—The person having the greatest number of votes for President, shall be the President, if such number be a majority of the whole number of Electors appointed; and if no person have such majority, then from the persons having the highest numbers not exceeding three on the list of those voted for as President, the House of Representatives shall chose immediately, by ballot, the President. But in choosing the President, the votes shall be taken by states, the representation from each state having one vote; a quorum for this purpose shall consist of a member or members from two-thirds of the states, and a majority of all the states shall be necessary to a choice. And if the House of Representatives shall not choose a President whenever the right of choice shall devolve upon them, before the fourth day of March next following, then the Vice-President shall act as President, as in the case of the death or other constitutional disability of the President.—The person having the greatest number of votes as Vice-President, shall be the Vice-President, if such number be a majority of the whole number

---

* Amended by the 20th Amendment, Sections 3 and 4.

of Electors appointed, and if no person have a majority, then from the two highest numbers on the list, the Senate shall choose the Vice-President; a quorum for the purpose shall consist of two-thirds of the whole number of Senators, and a majority of the whole number shall be necessary to a choice. But no person constitutionally ineligible to the office of President shall be eligible to that of Vice-President of the United States.

ARTICLE XIII

SECTION 1

Slavery prohibited

Neither slavery nor involuntary servitude, except as a punishment for crime whereof the party shall have been duly convicted, shall exist within the United States, or any place subject to their jurisdiction.

SECTION 2

Congress given power to enforce this article

Congress shall have power to enforce this article by appropriate legislation.

ARTICLE XIV

SECTION 1

Citizenship defined; privileges of citizens

All persons born or naturalized in the United States, and subject to the jurisdiction thereof, are citizens of the United States and of the State wherein they reside. No State shall make or enforce any law which shall abridge the privileges or immunities of citizens of the United States; nor shall any State deprive any person of life, liberty, or property, without due process of law; nor deny to any person within its jurisdiction the equal protection of the laws.

SECTION 2

Apportionment of Representatives

Representatives shall be apportioned among the several States according to their respective numbers, counting the whole number of persons in each State, excluding Indians not taxed. But when the right to vote at any election for the choice of electors for President and Vice-President of the United States, Representatives in Congress, the Executive and Judicial officers of a State, or the members of the Legislature thereof, is denied to any of the male inhabitants of such State, being twenty-one years of age, and citizens of the United States, or in any way abridged, except for participation in rebellion, or other crime, the basis of representation therein shall be reduced in the proportion which the number of such male citizens shall bear to the whole number of male citizens twenty-one years of age in such State.

SECTION 3

Disqualification for office; removal of disability

No person shall be a Senator or Representative in Congress, or elector of President and Vice President, or hold any office, civil or military, under the United States, or under any State, who, having previously taken an oath, as a member of Congress, or as an officer of the United States, or as a member of any State legislature, or as an executive or judicial officer of any State, to support the Constitution of the United States, shall have engaged in insurrection or rebellion against the same, or given aid or comfort to the enemies thereof. But Congress may by a vote of two-thirds of each House, remove such disability.

SECTION 4

Public debt not to be questioned; payment of debts and claims incurred in aid of rebellion forbidden

The validity of the public debt of the United States, authorized by law, including debts incurred for payment of pensions and bounties for services in suppressing insurrection or rebellion, shall not be questioned. But neither the United States nor any State shall assume or pay any debt or obligation incurred in aid of insurrection or rebellion against the United States, or any claim for the loss or emancipation of any slave; but all such debts, obligations and claims shall be held illegal and void.

SECTION 5

Congress given power to enforce this article

The Congress shall have power to enforce, by appropriate legislation, the provisions of this article.

ARTICLE XV

SECTION 1

Right of certain citizens to vote established

The right of citizens of the United States to vote shall not be denied or abridged by the United States or by any State on account of race, color, or previous condition of servitude.

SECTION 2

Congress given power to enforce this article

The Congress shall have power to enforce this article by appropriate legislation.

ARTICLE XVI

Taxes on income; Congress given power to lay and collect

The Congress shall have power to lay and collect taxes on incomes, from whatever source derived, without apportionment among the several states, and without regard to any census or enumeration.

ARTICLE XVII

Election of United States Senators; filling of vacancies; qualifications of electors

1. The Senate of the United States shall be composed of two Senators from each State, elected by the people thereof, for six years; and each Senator shall have one vote. The electors in each State shall have the qualifications requisite for electors of the most numerous branch of the State legislatures.

2. When vacancies happen in the representation of any State in the Senate, the executive authority of such State shall issue writs of election to fill such vacancies: *Provided,* That the legislature of any State may empower the executive thereof to make temporary appointment until the people fill the vacancies by election as the legislature may direct.

3. This amendment shall not be so construed as to affect the election or term of any Senator chosen before it becomes valid as part of the Constitution.

THE CONSTITUTION OF THE UNITED STATES

ARTICLE XVIII *

Manufacture, sale or transportation of intoxicating liquors, for beverage purposes, prohibited

1. After one year from the ratification of this article the manufacture, sale, or transportation of intoxicating liquors within, the importation thereof into, or the exportation thereof from the United States and all territory subject to the jurisdiction thereof for beverage purposes is hereby prohibited.

Congress and the several States given concurrent power to pass appropriate legislation to enforce this article

2. The Congress and the several States shall have concurrent power to enforce this article by appropriate legislation.

Provision of article to become operative, when adopted by three-fourths of the States

3. This article shall be inoperative unless it shall have been ratified as an amendment to the Constitution by the legislatures of the several States, as provided in the Constitution, within seven years from the date of the submission hereof to the States by the Congress.

ARTICLE XIX

The right of citizens to vote shall not be denied because of sex

The right of citizens of the United States to vote shall not be denied or abridged by the United States or by any States on account of sex.

Congress shall have power to enforce this article by appropriate legislation.

ARTICLE XX

SECTION 1

Terms of President, Vice-President, Senators and Representatives

The terms of the President and Vice-President shall end at noon on the twentieth day of January, and the terms of Senators and Representatives at noon on the third day of January, of the years in

---

* Repealed by the 21st Amendment.

which such terms would have ended if this article had not been ratified; and the terms of their successors shall then begin.

SECTION 2

Time of assembling Congress

The Congress shall assemble at least once in every year, and such meeting shall begin at noon on the third day of January, unless they shall by law appoint a different day.

SECTION 3

Filling vacancies in office of President

If, at the time fixed for the beginning of the term of the President, the President-elect shall have died, the Vice-President-elect shall become President. If a President shall not have been chosen before the time fixed for the beginning of his term, or if the President-elect shall have failed to qualify, then the Vice-President-elect shall act as President until a President shall have qualified; and the Congress may by law provide for the case wherein neither a President-elect nor a Vice-President-elect shall have qualified, declaring who shall then act as President, or the manner in which one who is to act shall be selected, and such person shall act accordingly until a President or Vice-President shall have qualified.

SECTION 4

Power of Congress in Presidential succession

The Congress may by law provide for the case of the death of any of the persons from whom the House of Representatives may choose a President whenever the right of choice shall have devolved upon them, and for the case of the death of any of the persons from whom the Senate may choose a Vice-President whenever the right of choice shall have devolved upon them.

SECTION 5

Time of taking effect

Sections 1 and 2 shall take effect on the 15th day of October following the ratification of this article.

THE CONSTITUTION OF THE UNITED STATES

SECTION 6

Ratification

This article shall be inoperative unless it shall have been ratified as an amendment to the Constitution by the legislatures of three-fourths of the several States within seven years from the date of its submission.

ARTICLE XXI

SECTION 1

Repeal of Prohibition Amendment

The eighteenth article of amendment to the Constitution of the United States is hereby repealed.

SECTION 2

Transportation of intoxicating liquors

The transportation or importation into any State, Territory, or possession of the United States for delivery or use therein of intoxicating liquors, in violation of the laws thereof, is hereby prohibited.

SECTION 3

Ratification

This article shall be inoperative unless it shall have been ratified as an amendment to the Constitution by conventions in the several States, as provided in the Constitution, within seven years from the date of the submission hereof to the States by the Congress.

ARTICLE XXII

SECTION 1

Limit to number of terms a President may serve

No person shall be elected to the office of the President more than twice, and no person who has held the office of President, or acted as President, for more than two years of a term to which some other person was elected President shall be elected to the office of the President more than once. But this Article shall not apply to any

person holding the office of President when this Article was proposed by the Congress, and shall not prevent any person who may be holding the office of President, or acting as President, during the term within which this Article becomes operative from holding the office of President or acting as President during the remainder of such term.

SECTION 2

Ratification

This article shall be inoperative unless it shall have been ratified as an amendment to the Constitution by the legislatures of three-fourths of the several States within seven years from the date of its submission to the States by the Congress.

ARTICLE XXIII

SECTION 1

Electors for the District of Columbia

The District constituting the seat of Government of the United States shall appoint in such manner as the Congress may direct:

A number of electors of President and Vice President equal to the whole number of Senators and Representatives in Congress to which the District would be entitled if it were a State, but in no event more than the least populous State; they shall be in addition to those appointed by the States, but they shall be considered, for the purposes of the election of President and Vice President, to be electors appointed by a State; and they shall meet in the District and perform such duties as provided by the twelfth article of amendment.

SECTION 2

Enforcement

The Congress shall have the power to enforce this article by appropriate legislation.

ARTICLE XXIV

SECTION 1

Citizens' Right to Vote in Federal Elections

The right of citizens of the United States to vote in any primary or other election for President or Vice President, for electors for

THE CONSTITUTION OF THE UNITED STATES

President or Vice President, or for Senator or Representative in Congress, shall not be denied or abridged by the United States or any State by reason of failure to pay any poll tax or other tax.

SECTION 2

The Congress shall have power to enforce this article by appropriate legislation.

ARTICLE XXV

SECTION 1

Filling the Offices of President or Vice President in Case of Vacancy

In case of the removal of the President from office or of his death or resignation, the Vice President shall become President.

SECTION 2

Whenever there is a vacancy in the office of the Vice President, the President shall nominate a Vice President who shall take office upon confirmation by a majority vote of both Houses of Congress.

SECTION 3

Whenever the President transmits to the President pro tempore of the Senate and the Speaker of the House of Representatives his written declaration that he is unable to discharge the powers and duties of his office, and until he transmits to them a written declaration to the contrary, such powers and duties shall be discharged by the Vice President as Acting President.

SECTION 4

Whenever the Vice President and a majority of either the principal officers of the executive departments or of such other body as Congress may by law provide, transmit to the President pro tempore of the Senate and the Speaker of the House of Representatives their written declaration that the President is unable to discharge the powers and duties of his office, the Vice President shall immediately assume the powers and duties of the office as Acting President.

Thereafter, when the President transmits to the President pro tempore of the Senate and the Speaker of the House of Representatives his written declaration that no inability exists, he shall resume the powers and duties of his office unless the Vice President and a majority of either the principal officers of the executive department or of such other body as Congress may by law provide, transmit within four days to the President pro tempore of the Senate and the Speaker of the House of Representatives their written declaration that the President is unable to discharge the powers and duties of his office. Thereupon Congress shall decide the issue, assembling within forty-eight hours for that purpose if not in session. If the Congress, within twenty-one days after the receipt of the latter written declaration, or, if Congress is not in session, within twenty-one days after Congress is required to assemble, determines by two-thirds vote of both Houses that the President is unable to discharge the powers and duties of his office, the Vice President shall continue to discharge the same as Acting President; otherwise, the President shall resume the powers and duties of his office.

RATIFICATION OF THE CONSTITUTION

The proposed Constitution was approved by the Convention on September 17, 1787, and was subsequently ratified by the several States, on the following dates: Delaware, December 7, 1787; Pennsylvania, December 12, 1787; New Jersey, December 18, 1787; Georgia, January 2, 1788; Connecticut, January 9, 1788; Massachusetts, February 6, 1788; Maryland, April 28, 1788; South Carolina, May 23, 1788; New Hampshire, June 21, 1788; Virginia, June 26, 1788; New York, July 26, 1788; North Carolina, November 21, 1789; Rhode Island, May 29, 1790.

(Ratification was effective when ratified by the ninth State—New Hampshire)

RELATING TO THE CONSTITUTION

O N June 28, 1787, when the Constitutional Convention found itself in great confusion and could not agree upon a course of action, the serene Benjamin Franklin arose in his place and addressed the President, George Washington:

"We have been assured, Sir, in the Sacred Writings, that— 'Except the Lord Build the House, they labor in vain that build it.' I firmly believe this; and I also believe that without His concurring aid, we shall succeed in this political building no better than the builders of Babel; we shall be divided in our little partial local interests, our projects will be confounded and we ourselves shall become a reproach and a bye word down to future ages. And what is worse, mankind may hereafter, from this unfortunate instance, despair of establishing Government by human wisdom and leave it to chance, war or conquest. I therefore beg leave to move—

"That henceforth, Prayers imploring the assistance of Heaven, and its blessings on our deliberations, be held in this Assembly every morning before we proceed to business, and that one or more of the clergy of this city be requested to officiate in that service."

The chairman of the convention that framed our Constitution was George Washington. On the back of his chair there was a painting of the sun as it appeared just above the horizon. When, after many months of wrangling and discussions which often threatened to break up the convention entirely, the Constitution was finally signed by the 39 delegates, Benjamin Franklin, then 83 years old, who had been a great stabilizing force in the convention, arose and said: "I have looked at that painting again and again. I have wondered whether it was a rising or a setting sun, but now I know it is a rising sun."

Now we must see to it that this sun that has shone upon us with such favor, that has seen America grow from a weak little group of colonies into the greatest of all nations, does not set.

RELATING TO THE CONSTITUTION

Writing the Constitution was a new task for men. And when they had finished it they described it as *"Novus ordo seclorum"*—the new order of the ages—as you will find engraved on your dollar bills, a quotation of Virgil nearly 2,000 years before. They wrought better than they knew, as all men know. For they had at last produced a balanced structure of power in which equality, justice, and liberty were in equilibrium.

The significant fact is that the American colonists fought and died to establish and preserve the principle of human freedom against what was then one of the greatest powers in the world. There were voices then, which told them they were weak, unprepared, not strong enough nor brave enough to challenge the power of the British Empire. These were the voices which counseled the ancient version of modern-day "peaceful co-existence." But the Founding Fathers did not listen. They knew for what they stood and were willing, if need be, to fight for it. It is well to remember that the cannonballs which exploded on Bunker Hill looked just as formidable and equally as destructive to our ancestors as a nuclear bomb does to us. But they knew that a principle is not successfully defended by the timid and the appeaser. And so they bequeathed to us a republic and a system that made us great, powerful and free. On that first American Independence Day a band of brave men "pledged their lives, their fortunes and their sacred honor" to the battle for human freedom. Can we do less?

With malice toward none, with charity for all, with firmness in the right as God gives us to see the right, let us strive on to finish the work we are in, to bind up the nation's wounds, to care for him who shall have borne the battle and for his widow and orphans, to do all which may achieve and cherish a just and a lasting peace among ourselves and with all nations.

—*Abraham Lincoln*

EXCERPTS FROM THE FEDERALIST, NO. 10

NOVEMBER 23, 1787

JAMES MADISON

THERE are two methods of curing the mischiefs of faction: the one, by removing its causes; the other by controlling its effects. . . .

The diversity in the faculties of men, from which the rights of property originate, is not less an insuperable obstacle to a uniformity of interests. The protection of these faculties is the first object of government. From the protection of different and unequal faculties of acquiring property, the possession of different degrees and kinds of property immediately results; and from the influence of these on the sentiments and views of the respective proprietors, ensues a division of the society into different interests and parties. . . .

But the most common and durable source of factions has been the various and unequal distribution of property. Those who hold and those who are without property have ever formed distinct interests in society. . . .

The inference to which we are brought is, that the *causes* of faction cannot be removed, and that relief is only to be sought in the means of controlling its *effects*.

If a faction consists of less than a majority, relief is supplied by the republican principle, which enables the majority to defeat its sinister views by regular vote. It may clog the administration, it may convulse the society; but it will be unable to execute and mask its violence under the forms of the Constitution. . . .

JAMES MADISON
1751 - 1836

EXCERPTS FROM WASHINGTON'S FAREWELL ADDRESS

UNITED STATES, SEPTEMBER 19, 1796
AFTER ANNOUNCING HIS RETIREMENT FROM PUBLIC LIFE,
PRESIDENT GEORGE WASHINGTON SAID:

. . . . Here, perhaps, I ought to stop. But a solicitude for your welfare . . . and the apprehension of danger, natural to that solicitude, urge me . . . to offer to your solemn contemplation, and to recommend to your frequent review, some sentiments; which are the result of much reflection, of no inconsiderable observation, and which appear to me all important to the permanency of your felicity as a People. These will be offered to you . . . as . . . the disinterested warnings of a parting friend, who can possibly have no personal motive to bias his counsel. . . .

Interwoven as is the love of liberty with every ligament of your hearts, no recommendation of mine is necessary to fortify or confirm the attachment.

The Unity of Government which constitutes you one people is also now dear to you. It is justly so; for it is a main Pillar in the Edifice of your real independence, the support of your tranquility at home; your peace abroad; of your safety; of your prosperity; of that very Liberty which you so highly prize. But as it is easy to foresee, that from different causes and from different quarters, much pains will be taken, many artifices employed, to weaken in your minds the conviction of this truth; as this is the point in your political fortress against which the batteries of internal and external enemies will be most constantly and actively (though often covertly and insidiously) directed, it is of infinite moment, that you should properly estimate the immense value of your national Union to your collective and individual happiness; that you should cherish a cordial, habitual and immoveable attachment to it; accustoming yourself to think and speak of it as of the Palladium of your political safety and prosperity; watching for its preservation with jealous anxiety; discountenancing whatever may suggest even a suspicion that it can in any event be abandoned, and indignantly frowning upon the first dawning of every attempt to alienate any portion of our Country from

52

the rest, or to enfeeble the sacred ties which now link together the various parts.

For this you have every inducement of sympathy and interest. Citizens by birth or choice, of a common country, that country has a right to concentrate your affections. The name of AMERICAN, which belongs to you . . . must always exalt the just pride of Patriotism, more than any appellation derived from local discriminations. With slight shades of difference, you have the same Religion, Manners, Habits and political Principles. You have in a common cause fought and triumphed together. The independence and liberty you possess are the work of joint councils, and joint efforts; of common dangers, sufferings and successes. . . .

In contemplating the causes wch. may disturb our Union, it occurs as matter of serious concern, that any ground should have been furnished for characterizing parties by *Geographical* discriminations: *Northern* and *Southern; Atlantic* and *Western;* whence designing men may endeavour to excite a belief that there is a real difference of local interests and views. One of the expedients of Party to acquire influence, within particular districts, is to misrepresent the opinions and aims of other Districts. You cannot shield yourselves too much against the jealousies and heart burnings which spring from these misrepresentations. They tend to render alien to each other those who ought to be bound together by fraternal affection. . . .

To the efficacy and permanency of Your Union, a Government for the whole is indispensable. . . . Sensible of this momentous truth, you have improved upon your first essay, by the adoption of a Constitution of Government, better calculated than your former for an intimate Union, and for the efficacious management of your common concerns. This government, the offspring of our own choice uninfluenced and unawed, adopted upon full investigation and mature deliberation, completely free in its principles, in the distribution of its powers, uniting security with energy, and containing within itself a provision for its own amendment, has a just claim to your confidence and your support. Respect for its authority, compliance with its Laws, acquiescence in its measures, are duties enjoined by the fundamental maxims of true Liberty. The basis of our political systems is the right of the people to make and to alter their Constitutions of Government. But the Constitution which at any time exists, 'till changed by an explicit and authentic act of the whole People, is sacredly obligatory upon all. The very idea of the power and the right of the People to establish

FROM WASHINGTON'S FAREWELL ADDRESS

Government presupposes the duty of every Individual to obey the established Government.

All obstructions to the execution of the Laws, all combinations and Associations, under whatever plausible character, with the real design to direct, controul, counteract, or awe the regular deliberation and action of the constituted authorities are destructive of this fundamental principle and of fatal tendency. They serve to organize faction, to give it an artificial and extraordinary force; to put in the place of the delegated will of the Nation, the will of a party; often a small but artful and enterprizing minority of the community; and, according to the alternate triumphs of different parties, to make the public administration the mirror of the ill concerted and incongruous projects of faction, rather than the Organ of consistent and wholesome plans digested by common councils and modefied by mutual interests. However combinations or associations of the above description may now and then answer popular ends, they are likely, in the course of time and things, to become potent engines, by which cunning, ambitious and unprincipled men will be enabled to subvert the Power of the People, and to usurp for themselves the reins of Government; destroying afterwards the very engines which have lifted them to unjust dominion.

Towards the preservation of your Government and the permanency of your present happy state, it is requisite, not only that you steadily discountenance irregular oppositions to its acknowledged authority, but also that you resist with care the spirit of innovation upon its principles however specious the pretexts. One method of assault may be to effect, in the forms of the Constitution, alterations which will impair the energy of the system, and thus to undermine what cannot be directly overthrown. In all the changes to which you may be invited, remember that time and habit are at least as necessary to fix the true character of Governments, as of other human institutions; that experience is the surest standard, by which to test the real tendency of the existing Constitution of a coun'ry; that facility in changes upon the credit of mere hypotheses and opinion exposes to perpetual change, from the endless variety of hypotheses and opinion: and remember, especially, that for the efficient management of your common interests, in a country so extensive as ours, a Government of as much vigour as is consistent with the perfect security of Liberty is indispensable. Liberty itself will find in such a Government, with powers properly distributed and adjusted, its surest Guardian. It is indeed little else than a name, where the Government is too feeble to withstand the enterprises of faction, to confine each member of the Society within the limits prescribed by the laws and to maintain all in the secure and tranquil enjoyment of the rights of person and property. . . .

Let me now take a more comprehensive view, and warn you in the most solemn manner against the baneful effects of the Spirit of Party, generally.

This Spirit, unfortunately, is inseperable from our nature, having its root in the strongest passions of the human mind. It exists under different shapes in all Governments, more or less stifled, controuled, or repressed; but in those of the popular form it is seen in its greatest rankness and is truly their worst enemy.

The alternate dominion of one faction over another, sharpened by the spirit of revenge natural to party dissention, which in different ages and countries has perpetrated the most horrid enormities, is itself a frightful despotism. But this leads at length to a more formal and permanent despotism. The disorders and miseries, which result, gradually incline the minds of men to seek security and repose in the absolute power of an Individual: and sooner or later the chief of some prevailing faction more able or more fortunate than his competitors, turns this disposition to the purposes of his own elevation, on the ruins of Public Liberty. . . .

The common and continual mischiefs of the spirit of Party are sufficient to make it the interest and the duty of a wise People to discourage and restrain it.

It is important, likewise, that the habits of thinking in a free Country should inspire caution in those entrusted with its administration, to confine themselves within their respective Constitutional spheres; avoiding in the exercise of the Powers of one department to encroach upon another. The spirit of encroachment tends to consolidate the powers of all the departments in one, and thus to create whatever the form of government, a real despotism. A just estimate of that love of power, and proneness to abuse it, which predominates in the human heart is sufficient to satisfy us of the truth of this position. The necessity of reciprocal checks in the exercise of political power; by dividing and distributing it into different depositories, and constituting each the Guardian of the Public Weal against invasions by the others, has been evinced by experiments ancient and modern; some of them in our country and under our own eyes. To preserve them must be as necessary as to institute them. If in the opinion of the People, the distribution or modification of the Constitutional powers be in any particular wrong, let it be corrected by an amendment in the way which the Constitution designates. But let there be no change by usurpation; for though this, in one instance, may be the instrument of good, it is the customary weapon by which free governments are destroyed. The precedent must always greatly overbalance in permanent evil any partial or transient benefit which the use can at any time yield.

Of all the dispositions and habits which lead to political prosperity, Religion and morality are indispensable supports. In vain would that man claim the tribute of Patriotism, who should labour to subvert these great Pillars of human happiness, these firmest props of the duties of Men and citizens. . . . Let it simply be asked where is the security for property, for reputation, for life, if the sense of religious obligation *desert* the oaths, which are the instruments of investigation in Courts of Justice? And let us with caution indulge the supposition, that morality can be maintained without religion. Whatever may be conceded to the influence of refined education on minds of peculiar structure, reason and experience both forbid us to expect that National morality can prevail in exclusion of religious principle.

'Tis substantially true, that virtue or morality is a necessary spring of popular government. . . . Who that is a sincere friend to it, can look with indifference upon attempts to shake the foundation of the fabric?

Promote then as an object of primary importance, Institutions for the general diffusion of knowledge. In proportion as the structure of a government gives force to public opinion, it is essential that public opinion should be enlightened.

As a very important source of strength and security, cherish public credit. One method of preserving it is to use it as sparingly as possible: avoiding occasions of expence by cultivating peace, but remembering also that timely disbursements to prepare for danger frequently prevent much greater disbursements to repel it; avoiding likewise the accumulation of debt, not only by shunning occasions of expence, but by vigorous exertions in time of Peace to discharge the Debts which unavoidable wars may have occasioned, not ungenerously throwing upon posterity the burthen which we ourselves ought to bear. The execution of these maxims belongs to your Representatives, but it is necessary that public opinion should cooperate. To facilitate to them the performance of their duty, it is essential that you should practically bear in mind, that towards the payment of debts there must be Revenue; that to have Revenue there must be taxes; that no taxes can be devised which are not more or less inconvenient and unpleasant; that the intrinsic embarrassment inseperable from the selection of the proper objects (which is always a choice of difficulties) ought to be a decisive motive for a candid construction of the conduct of the Government in making it, and for a spirit of acquiescence in the measures for obtaining Revenue which the public exigencies may at any time dictate.

Observe good faith and justice towards all Nations. Cultivate peace and harmony with all. Religion and morality enjoin this conduct; and can it be that good policy does not equally enjoin it? It will be worthy of a free, enlightened, and, at no distant period, a great Nation, to give to mankind the magnanimous and too novel example of a People always guided by an exalted justice and benevolence. Who can doubt that in the course of time and things the fruits of such a plan would richly repay any temporary advantages which might be lost by a steady adherence to it? Can it be, that Providence has not connected the permanent felicity of a Nation with its virtue? . . .

Against the insidious wiles of foreign influence, (I conjure you to believe me fellow citizens) the jealousy of a free people ought to be *constantly* awake; since history and experience prove that foreign influence is one of the most baneful foes of Republican Government. But that jealousy to be useful must be impartial; else it becomes the instrument of the very influence to be avoided, instead of a defence against it. Excessive partiality for one foreign nation and excessive dislike of another, cause those whom they actuate to see danger only on one side, and serve to veil and even second the arts of influence on the other. Real Patriots, who may resist the intriegues of the favourite, are liable to become suspected and odious; while its tools and dupes usurp the applause and confidence of the people, to surrender their interests.

The Great rule of conduct for us, in regard to foreign Nations is in extending our commercial relations to have with them as little *political* connection as possible. So far as we have already formed engagements let them be fulfilled, with perfect good faith. Here let us stop.

FROM WASHINGTON'S FAREWELL ADDRESS

Europe has a set of primary interests, which to us have none, or a very remote relation. . . . Hence therefore it must be unwise in us to implicate ourselves, by artificial ties, in the ordinary vicissitudes of her politics, or the ordinary combinations and collisions of her friendships, or enmities: . . .

'Tis our true policy to steer clear of permanent alliances, with any portion of the foreign world—so far, I mean, as we are now at liberty to do it, for let me not be understood as capable of patronising infidility to existing engagements (I hold the maxim no less applicable to public than to private affairs that honesty is always the best policy). . . .

Taking care always to keep ourselves, by suitable establishments, on a respectably defensive posture, we may safely trust to temporary alliances for extraordinary emergencies.

Harmony, liberal intercourse with all Nations, are recommended by policy, humanity and interest. But even our commercial policy should hold an equal and impartial hand: neither seeking nor granting exclusive favours or preferences; consulting the natural course of things; diffusing and diversifying by gentle means the streams of commerce, but forcing nothing; establishing with Powers so disposed—in order to give to trade a stable course, to define the rights of our Merchants, and to enable the Government to support them—conventional rules of intercourse; the best that present circumstances and mutual opinion will permit, but temporary, and liable to be from time to time abandoned or varied, as experience and circumstances shall dictate; constantly keeping in view, that 'tis folly in one Nation to look for disinterested favors from another; that it must pay with a portion of its Independence for whatever it may accept under that character; that by such acceptance, it may place itself in the condition of having given equivalents for nominal favours and yet of being reproached with ingratitude for not giving more. There can be no greater error than to expect, or calculate upon real favours from Nation to Nation. . . .

In offering to you, my Countrymen, these counsels of an old and affectionate friend, I dare not hope they will make the strong and lasting impression, I could wish. . . . But if . . . they may now and then recur to moderate the fury of party spirit, to warn against the mischiefs of foreign Intriegue, to guard against the Impostures of pretended patriotism; this hope will be a full recompence for the solicitude for your welfare, by which they have been dictated. . . .

58

THE AMERICAN'S CREED

I BELIEVE in the United States of America as a Government of the people, by the people, for the people; whose just powers are derived from the consent of the governed; a democracy in a republic; a sovereign nation of many sovereign states; a perfect union, one and inseparable; established upon those principles of freedom, equality, justice, and humanity for which American patriots sacrificed their lives and fortunes.

I therefore believe it is my duty to my country to love it; to support its Constitution; to obey its laws; to respect its flag; and to defend it against all enemies.

William Tyler Page

Courtesy The Freedoms Foundation at Valley Forge

GENERAL WASHINGTON AT PRAYER

60

COMMUNISM—
ENEMY
OF ALL
FREEDOMS

by

ROBERT B. WATTS, 33°, G∴C∴
Director of Education

TABLE OF CONTENTS

KNOW YOUR COMMUNIST ENEMY

INTRODUCTION

Mr. J. Edgar Hoover, Director of the Federal Bureau of Investigation and one of the world's most outstanding authorities on Communism, has written:

"This nation is face to face with the gravest danger ever to confront it. The menace of Communism is no simple, forthright threat. It is a sinister and deadly conspiracy which can be conquered by an alert, informed citizenry dedicated to the preservation of the principles on which America was founded."

Mr. Hoover is supported by the nation's only surviving five-star general, Gen. Omar N. Bradley. Speaking at the National Press Club in Washington, D. C., on March 3, 1970, General Bradley laid the present situation right on the line when he said:

"Maybe our people do not understand what faces us. Maybe you gentlemen (newsmen) have not hit the guts of the problem, or have not hit hard enough.

"I believe our greatest danger is still imperialist communism and those Communist countries which wish to spread their domination throughout the world under the guise of Communist Utopia.

"We see their methods of accomplishing their aims by so-called brush fire wars such as Korea and Vietnam, and by outright invasion such as in Hungary and Czechoslovakia and even by infiltration of our own society.

"I think it is naive to believe that all the groups of which we read, advocating the overthrow by force of our present systems and government, are unrelated outbreaks of spontaneous political thought."

It is the purpose of this booklet to assist in informing every American of the nature and extent of this threat to freedoms everywhere in the world and to our country in particular.

The proof of what Communism is, what is stands for, and how it relentlessly uses people and then degrades them, using wholesale murder as a way of maintaining itself, is written in bold letters both by what it says and by what it has done.

Every free person everywhere, and especially in the United States of America, should read the truth about Communism and then ask himself or herself, "Is that what I want for myself, or my family, or my Country?"

4

HOW COMMUNISM BEGAN

For generations, Russia—with its vast area extending over about half of Europe and the northern half of Asia, and with a population of some 175,000,000—had been ruled with an iron hand by the Tsars.

Great luxury enjoyed by the rich was matched by great poverty among the people. And the latter had no voice whatever in their government and scant freedom, save in matters of religion, in respect to themselves. Brutality was common in dealing with the people.

An example of this brutality occurred on January 22, 1905. On that day, known thereafter as "Red Sunday," starving Russians appeared before the palace of the Tsars to recite their woes to the one to whom they affectionately referred as the "Little Father of all the Russias." Instead they were met by Cossacks, hard riding cavalrymen who used their whips on the mass of pleading citizens. Then the palace guard fired into the crowd, cutting down defenseless men, women and children. There was no audience with the Tsar.

But in 1917, the Empire of the Tsars was overthrown by its people who sought the right to govern themselves.

One of the first things which any observer of Communism should know is that the Communists had no part in this freedom-seeking revolution. In fact, the Romanoff dynasty of Tsars began to weaken a dozen years before when the Russian navy was annihilated and 60,000 of the nation's soldiers fell in one fateful battle of the War with Japan. Disaster fell at home as well as at the front. There was famine, and domestic affairs were dishonestly and ineffectively administered.

This continuing weakness of power and increase of corruption in the administration of internal affairs finally resulted in 1915 in the successful uprising of the people and the end of the rule of the Tsars. Unlike the situation which had prevailed at the "Red Sunday" massacre, this time the workmen who massed to voice their discontent to the Tsar of that time were not defenseless. Soldiers, some of them stragglers from the German-Russian line then moving stubbornly toward Petrograd in World War I, came to the rescue of the workers and turned their guns against the Government.

Tsar Nicholas II abdicated in favor of his brother, but the latter refused to attempt to continue the Empire.

THE DEMOCRATIC
PROVISIONAL GOVERNMENT

The court of the Romanoffs thus overthrown was often brilliant, often corrupt, sometimes both, but never responsive to the will of the people. It is not difficult to understand, therefore, that the Russian people in 1917, convinced that the "bad old days were gone forever," were jubilant when a Provisional Government formed under Prime Minister Alexander Kerensky following the abdication, seemed to assure an end to more than three centuries of oppression. Indeed, it might be said that all the freedom loving peoples of the world figuratively breathed a sigh of relief at this turn of events. At this point in the drama of Russian history Nicolai Lenin, literally from the left wing, stepped on the stage.

It is worth emphasizing again that Communism played practically no part in the people's revolt which had freedom as its objective. The short-lived attempt on the part of the Russian people to establish a truly democratic type of government was made by what the Communists derisively called "the bourgeoisie"—property owners, employers, capitalists, professional people and some of the nobility, aided by the people. What the Communists did do was to destroy the Provisional Government established by these Communist-hated classes, and thus kill the only attempt at self-rule ever experienced by the Russian people. Thus from its very inception, Communism has stood as the deadly enemy of all freedoms in government and in personal liberty, wherever in the world they exist. It continues to be that deadly enemy today.

Returning to the events which followed the overthrow of the Tsars and set up a free democratic Provisional Government of the people, we see that in one of its first acts the Provisional Government invited the political refugees from the Romanoffs to come back home, and pledged the support of Russia to the Allies against the Central Powers in World War I. The German General, Erick Ludendorff, hoping Lenin would somehow get the Russians off the Eastern Front so he could move to the West the German soldiers in position there, whisked Lenin and some of his aides across Germany in a sealed railroad car. Thus Lenin made his way home through Sweden and Finland; Trotsky returned from New York City; Stalin came back from his Siberian prison camp, and the three Communist "greats" were together and soon to unite in crushing the free Provisional Government.

6

THE DEATH OF THE PROVISIONAL GOVERNMENT

Now let us see how ruthless Communism achieved that end. It is a typical example of how Communism works when it gets the chance. Trotsky's task was to organize and arm the members of the relatively small Communist groups which these three stalwarts had helped to gain a foothold in the nation. Upon his return Lenin was welcomed by the Russian people as one whom the Provisional Government had saved from banishment. Far from expressing gratitude for this kindness, Lenin, working with Trotsky in a campaign of destructive oratory, thundered against the democratic ideals of the new system which the Provisional Government was trying to build. We hear the same shrill cries today.

Stalin, a good writer, used pamphlets to blast the free Government. The three of them called for the removal of the leaders of the Provisional Government and for a "dictatorship of the proletariat." Their slogan was "Bread, Peace and Freedom," three of the goods things of life which it would be difficult to argue against at any time, and certainly not at a time when Russian casualties were mounting to 8,500,000 men in a war which they were losing, when the people were not sufficiently fed, and where the land was held largely under feudal tenure.

The Communist campaign was swift. It began in November, 1917. The first step was Lenin's order to Trotsky to have his soldiers fire on the Winter Palace where the officials of the Provisional Government had established themselves when Tsar Nicholas II had abandoned it.

The Provisional Government, consistent with its plans for true democratic government by the people, had set January 18, 1918, for the meeting of a representative assembly elected by the citizens. Most of the delegates elected were opposed to a dictatorship of the proletariat. They had had enough of dictators, and wanted freedom for their people and their country. Lenin knew he could not depend upon them for support. So without any authority he created his own "Congress of Soviets," members of which were recruited from small Communist groups. He then boldly proclaimed this Congress to be the true assembly of the people.

When the real delegates chosen in the election held by the citizens under the terms of the Provisional Government took their seats on the above date, they looked down the barrels of rifles of the Red Guard.

7

THE DEATH OF THE PROVISIONAL GOVERNMENT

They dispersed and the "Soviet Congress" took their place. The Russian plan to build a free and democratic government was dead.

Communism had claimed its first huge victory over Freedom. It has never ceased to attempt to extend that victory and to destroy freedoms all over the world.

WHAT COMMUNISM STANDS FOR

No one has to guess about the beliefs, the aims or the purposes of Communism. And no one has to be fooled by claims of the high ideals of the Reds. The truth is in writing for anyone to read for himself.

The basic doctrine and beliefs of Communism are set out clearly in "The Communist Manifesto," written in 1848 by Karl Marx—a man previously deported from Russia, France and Belgium—and by Friedrich Engels, a German living at the time in England, as was Marx.

Fundamentally, as the Manifesto states, "The Communists everywhere support revolutionary movement against the existing social and political order of things." Quoting again, "The Communists - - - openly declare that their ends can be attained only by the forcible overthrow of all existing social conditions. Let the ruling classes tremble at a Communist revolution." Again, "- - - the theory of the Communists may be summed up in the simple sentence: Abolition of private property." And finally, "Communism abolishes eternal truths, it abolishes all religion and all morality, instead of constituting them on a new basis; it, therefore, acts in contradiction to all past historical experience."

Compare these official objectives with a statement which appeared in an article entitled "Toward a Revolutionary Student Movement" by Doug Kennell, of the University of California, in "Pine Tree" magazine (Spring 1970).

> "It is a struggle for the right of every individual to choose how he shall live as a social being. The revolution will not end with the establishment of a new social system, but with the disestablishment of all compulsory social systems."

Supporting these and similar doctrines and beliefs of Communism are Marx's basic theory that men are the victims of their material environment only, and may be manipulated by changing that environment; and that in order to accomplish this end there must be a "dictatorship of the proletariat" to command and achieve the ultimate perfect State.

The dictatorship established in the Soviet Union is however, not the dictatorship demanded by Marx and planned by Lenin—a dictatorship of the working people. It is a dictatorship exercised by the few men who control the Communist Party. This shift was made by Stalin, who tightened the screws of his dictatorship by saying that "- - - the dictatorship of the proletariat is in essence the dictatorship of its vanguard, the dictatorship of its party, as the main guiding force of the proletariat."

Thus the destinies of some 200 million people in the Soviet Union are theoretically in the hands of the three or four percent of their number who have been accepted into the Communist Party, but actually are in the hands of the top leaders of Red Russia who control the party by dealing swift death or banishment to any who oppose them.

Every top Soviet leader has been quick to use terror and annihilation to maintain his absolute power over the Soviet Communist party, the nation and its conquered lands.

One of the bloodiest of Communism's ruthless dealings with any whom it fancies to be an enemy or even a potential enemy was begun by Stalin on December 1, 1934. His aim was the literal extermination of any who he regarded as an opponent.

In a speech long kept secret, which was delivered to the Twentieth Congress of the Communist Party in 1956, Nikita Khrushchev, who had loyally supported Stalin in his butcheries but later turned against him politically, flatly stated that, "Of 139 members and candidates of the Party's Central Committee (a top control group) 98 persons, i.e., 70% were arrested and shot (by Stalin's orders). The same fate met a majority of the delegates to the Seventeenth Congress. Of 1,966 delegates - - - 1,108 persons were arrested on charges of counterrevolutionary crimes" (and shot). And according to Georg von Rauch in "A History of Soviet Russia," not only was the heavy majority of party members wiped out, but "According to conservative estimates about seven to eight million people—according to others, twenty-three million—became victims of this purge."

In Russia itself, many of the large-scale projects of the state such as highways, canals, dams and mines have been manned by labor slaves forced to work without pay as punishment for alleged crime, for unfaithfulness to the Communist Party, for violation of work laws, or for resisting the collectivization of their property. The victims include prisoners of war and citizens of the Soviet satellites who opposed the imposition of Communism on their countries. The American Federation of Labor estimates that there were 15,000,000 Russian labor slaves in 1952.

This ruthless disregard of human life and dignity carries right down to every person in a Communist-controlled country.

10

RELICS OF COMMUNIST SAVAGERY

This photograph of items recovered from the bodies of Polish officers, found by an United States House of Representatives Committee headed by Honorable Ray J. Madden, M. C., to have been massacred by Soviet Communists, is presented from the official exhibits of the Committee.

WHAT COMMUNISM STANDS FOR

In House Report 2505, 82nd Congress, 2nd Session, Congressman Ray J. Madden of Indiana, Chairman, filed a Final Report on what is characterized therein as "one of the most barbarous international crimes in world history." It "involved some 4,243 of the 15,400 Polish Army officers and intellectual leaders who were captured by the Soviets when Russia invaded Poland in September 1939," and is known as "the Katyn massacre."

By an interim report of this unprecedented and courageous House Committee, filed on July 2, 1952, "it fixed the guilt for the Katyn massacre on the Soviet NKVD, People's Commissariat of Internal Affairs."

Perhaps the meat of the 2,362 pages of this outstanding American inquiry is contained in the Committee's following sentence:

"Katyn was a means to an end. The Soviets had plotted to take over Poland as early as 1939. Their massacre of these Polish officers was designed to eliminate the intellectual leadership which subsequently would have attempted to block Russia's ultimate designs for complete communization of Poland. This was but a step of the Soviets toward the complete communization of Europe and eventually the entire world, including the United States." (Italics in original.)

Speaking at Washington, D. C., on April 7, 1970, Congressman Madden drove home the present day pertinence of his Committee's report. He said, "I might say to some of the younger folks in this country who are becoming enamored with this organized Communist propaganda in colleges and other places, that if the Communists ever took over they also might be among those massacred." Continuing, he said "Human life means no more than pebbles on a beach to these people. Wiping out millions of lives to gain their ends is nothing to them. Let the Communists take over and there would be no meetings, no freedom, no anything which free men cherish!"

To the Marxist, morals, ethics, integrity, honor and honesty are merely words invented by an exploiting class to indicate certain methods of human behavior which will contribute to the achievement of the objectives of the exploiters.

Indicative of this total disregard for truth, honor or integrity are Lenin's words in the Party Platform for 1919: "We will use any ruses, dodges, tricks, cunning, unlawful methods, concealment and veiling of the truth." It was also Lenin who said "Promises are like pie crusts— made to be broken." Pursuant to this philosophy, the course of Soviet

12

history is strewn with the wreckage of broken international agreements and treaties, great and small.

As Mr. J. Edgar Hoover puts it, "Soviet history is replete with instances of - - - treachery. A United States Senate report of the study of nearly one thousand treaties showed that in 38 years the Soviet Union had violated agreements with practically every nation to which it had given its solemn, written pledge."

How any intelligent person can know these facts about what the Communists have done in Russia and in other countries held captive by Russia, and not be turned completely against this menace, is hard to understand. Perhaps in part it is the old story that, "It happened in Russia but it can't happen here."

Millions of people have thought that about their countries, and have died for their mistake, or lost every ounce of their human dignity and all of their freedoms.

Again, all anyone has to do is to read history and look for himself.

THE COMMUNIST OFFENSIVE

So far, the Communist Party has never relaxed this type of merciless grip as a dictator, wherever it has achieved power. Again we see the real issue to be between freedom wherever it exists anywhere in the world, and the iron fist of Communist domination which crushes freedoms. Any who dare to "deviate" from Communist belief, once they are conquered, do so at peril of their lives.

One of America's greatest military men, who has faced and studied Communism in wide areas of the world, General Lyman L. Lemnitzer, U.S.A. (Rtd.), joins in pointing to the "- - - well-known Communist objective repeatedly and emphatically stated by every Soviet leader for the last fifty years—Communist world domination under Soviet direction and control."

The chilling accuracy of this statement is to be found in an examination of what Communism, the dictatorship, has done in the years since its killing of democracy in Russia in 1917.

We present here the list of nations which, up to the time of going to press, have been conquered by Communism, together with the year when that was accomplished. The black borders are symbolic of the literal death of all freedoms in those countries—death which has been brought by Communism, the enemy of all freedoms everywhere.

Let no one think for one minute, after reading the following list of conquered nations, that "it can't happen here."

Instead, let him read in sober contemplation of *what has happened,* the warning which was given to the world in 1947 by Aleksandr F. Kerensky:

"The myth that the Communists overthrew czarism has been purposely spread to conceal their crime of having strangled the first Russian democracy. And today Communists everywhere are trying to seize power by the same cynical device: posing as 'defenders of democracy,' organizing their blows against liberty under the banners of liberty. It was not until after his victory that Lenin admitted publicly that his freedom-loving slogans had been deliberate deception.

The Russian people cannot be blamed for falling into the Bolshevik trap for, at that time, the world had had no experience

14

THE COMMUNIST OFFENSIVE

with modern totalitarian techniques. But there is no such excuse for the millions of workers, farmers and intellectuals in the democratic West who are offered the bait today. To them the frightful experience of my native land should serve as a grim warning."

Name	Year
RUSSIA	1917
NORTH CAUCASIA	1920
IDEL-URAL	1920
COSSACKIA	1920
AZERBAIJAN	1920
ARMENIA	1920
BYLO-RUSSIA	1920
SOVIET GEORGIA	1921
FAR EASTERN-REPUBLIC	1922
TURKISTAN	1922
THE UKRAINE	1922
POLAND	1939
LITHUANIA	1940
LATVIA	1940
ESTONIA	1940
ALBANIA	1944
EAST GERMANY	1945
CHINA	1945-1949
YUGOSLAVIA	1946
CZECHOSLOVAKIA	1948
RUMANIA	1948
BULGARIA	1948
HUNGARY	1949
TIBET	1951
NORTH KOREA	1953
NORTH VIETNAM	1954
CUBA	1959

(Data courtesy The Freedoms Foundation at Valley Forge)

HOW COMMUNISM CONQUERS

In 1955, the American Bar Association issued the following statement:

> "For those who want to understand Communism, we prescribe not a fifteen day trip to Russia, but fifteen days in a library studying the Communist Conspiracy."

What these men are saying is, of course, that so much time has passed since the first Communist treachery of 1917, and so many nations—27 up to 1970, representing some 40% of the earth's surface—have undergone Communist dictator domination, that anyone can find in a library a description of just how the Communist conspiracy to conquer the world has operated time after time.

As was stated earlier, it is the purpose of this booklet to present in simple form exactly that information.

Communism uses every conceivable method in attempting to overthrow free governments and conquer them. Whatever methods seem most likely to be successful in a given case will be used, either singly or in series. However, there are nine classic steps used in one way or another in achieving the take-over of a target country. The history books reveal them in detail.

STEP 1

Since the shortest distance between two points is a straight line, an obvious first technique is by direct, massive military power which results at once in the desired Communist take-over. Examples of the destruction of people's freedoms and governments by this means are to be found in the Baltic States.

Johannes Klesment, former member of the Estonia Ministry of Justice, describes the direct approach against his country in these simple words:

> "At that time large Soviet military forces were stationed on the Estonian border, and Soviet military planes were flying over Estonian territory. Acceptance of the Soviet ultimatum was inevitable. Estonia, with a population of only 1¼ million, could not oppose the Soviet military forces, especially in 1939, when it had no hope of getting military aid from the Western countries."

16

(From Study for the Senate Committee on the Judiciary, 89th Congress, 2nd Session.)

A variant of this method is by the frequently-used technique of encirclement. Many of the conquered nations were overcome by creating a fierce ring of external pressure, applied through the presence just outside their borders of massive Communist military forces. Inside, there are brought to bear any one or all of six other Steps, all designed to lead up to a contrived crisis which is used as the occasion for an ultimate demand for majority representation by Communists in the encircled government. Once this demand is granted, the kill has been made.

A favorite means of reaching this final point in an encircled country is the device of persuading a target nation to enter unto a coalition government in which Communism has some representatives. East-Central Europe offers classic examples of this technique.

Next follow radical reforms and arrests for asserted conspiracies against the existing regime, the broadest type of subversion and ultimate Communist control of key sources of power and influence, and lastly a carefully contrived crisis in which the coalition government is replaced by a government chosen wholly by the Communists.

As stated in a 1966 report to a Sub-Committee of the Committee on the Judiciary of the United States Senate (89th Congress, 2nd Session):

"Past experiences show that the Communists exploit their presence in governing bodies to foster their ultimate objective of seizing total power, followed by liquidation of all opposition, suppression of freedom of the press, speech and worship, and transformation of a country into a totalitarian police state."

Those words are worth re-reading!

STEP 2

Always used to the utmost advantage is the saturation of a target country with propaganda.

Some three billion dollars a year are used for such propaganda in the United States alone—always masked as to its source, and frequently unsuspected of being propaganda. Here the purpose is to subvert such groups as the clergy, the teachers and the students at all academic levels.

The basic bait used is the call upon such groups to accept a role of active leadership in the solution of the ills of the world—they being told that such leaders are required to lead the people to bright new lives

17

which will be planned and achieved under the Communists. Many are taken in by this flattery—and see themselves as their country's leaders after the destruction of the present government and the resulting Soviet take-over. In fact, of course, these dupes are used only so long as they are useful and then they are dropped or liquidated. None ever survive to bask in leadership after their country falls.

Much propaganda is also used to influence internal dissent in any field possible. And much is used to deny, explain or rationalize the violent actions of Communists elsewhere in the world.

More and more the use of this device is becoming visible throughout the United States, with mob violence directed almost as obviously as an orchestra is led, and with more and more open communication between Communist countries and those who are active in the current mass agitations being revealed. Financing pours in for the most vicious radicals, and asylum is extended in Communist areas when escape from punishment is needed.

No regard, of course, is paid to the actual facts in preparing this propaganda. It is but a tool used in attempting to conquer the world.

STEP 3

This step involves the creation within the target country of mass agitation. Any issues at hand are used.

Stirring up hatred and violence between races is especially sought after because of the deep divisions which such strife creates. Civil turmoil over religion is encouraged for the same reason. Widespread stoppages of work, laborers' violence on picket lines, the demoralizing of essential city services such as refuse removal, and the furnishing of water, electricity and gas are all diligently encouraged.

In short, this is the old device of "divide and conquer."

In Czechoslovakia, for example, the United States Senate document quoted above states:

"- - - the Communists followed a tactic of conflict, infiltration, sabotage and subversion. In their effort, they were assisted by the diplomatic representatives, delegations and official propaganda of the Soviet Union."

Student riots are important parts and parcels of this technique, and have been seen all over the world where Communism has been or is seeking domination. As a matter of fact, student riots were an integral part of the Russian revolution itself—complete with the "hippies" of that day, the rejection of all moral codes and the widespread use of drugs. Such things are really "old hat" to the Communists, if our young people only knew it.

STEP 4

This is the process of infiltration.

Communists have always been in the minority. They often win despite that fact because they are perfectly organized, are absolutely subject to following orders, and make a point of gaining access to areas of influence. Once one gets in, he opens the door for others.

This process is part of the espionage activity of the Communists.

Its representatives to the United Nations, assured free entry into the United States by the presence here of the United Nations headquarters, are to an overwhelming extent direct operatives of the Russian intelligence service. Its embassies and consulates, using diplomatic immunity to the fullest, are known centers of espionage. Comparable access to the Soviet Union on the part of the free world is, however, non-existent.

Every American knows some of the results of this espionage, if no more than the story of the stealing of our nuclear weapon secrets. But the effort is constant and almost without limit.

An estimate by the United States Department of State indicates that for many years there have been, throughout the world, some 300,000 trained officers serving in the 27 intelligence and security services of the Communist-bloc nations.

STEP 5

This is the technique of demoralization.

Sometimes it is superficially called the "scare technique," illustrated by such slogans as "Better Red than Dead"—although the truth of that slogan may be highly debatable.

Really, the matter goes much further and has been better described by the Communist strategists themselves as "the Trojan Horse technique."

What is that technique, and how does it operate?

For the beginning of an answer, let us read the words of Lenin himself, one of those who destroyed the Russian attempt to create a democratic people's government and at muzzle point replaced it with Communism. Lenin said:

> "It is possible to conquer the more powerful enemy only by exerting the utmost effort, and by necessarily, thoroughly, care-

fully, attentively and skillfully taking advantage of every, even the smallest, fissure among the enemies, of every antagonism of interest among the bourgeoisie in the various countries; by taking advantage of every, even the smallest opportunity of gaining a mass ally, even though this ally may be temporary, vacillating, unstable, unreliable, and conditional. Those who do not understaand this fail to understand even a grain of Marxism and of scientific, modern socialism in general. Those who have not proved by deeds over a considerable period of time, and in sufficiently varied political situations, their ability to apply this truth in practice, have not yet learned to assist the revolutionary class in its struggle for the emancipation of the whole of toiling humanity from the exploiters.

It is of particular importance to Americans to know about this theory, since our country has for some time been one of its prime targets. Let us, therefore, look about us. What is happening here which might affect our ability and willingness to fight when the final assault is made on us?

Already the atheistic enemy and its followers and dupes have established a bridgehead in the so-called "New Theology" whose phophets loudly declaim that "God is dead." Books are written, magazines report the sayings and doings of these blasphemous atheists, and until lately, few were the voices which were raised in protest. But this attack upon religion has already run most of its course. The sensationalists have written their books, many of the beguiled clergy have given up their antics in the face of solid disapproval by their congregations, and the sure instinct of most people that the spiritual must always prevail over the material has asserted itself.

Then we have the "New Morality," whose proponents would sweep away the old moral codes in a sea of license. This has always been the objective of Communism, which instinctively knows that if it can deprive men and women of decency, they can more easily stomach the inhumanity of the Communist way of life. As Mr. Hoover says:

"The philosophy of Communism flourishes best in an environment where personal responsibility and self-discipline have been undermined by immorality, materialism and expedience."

Could you ask for a more undermining philosophy than the "New Morality" if you wanted to try to sell Communism? And remember that Communism's dedication to both atheism and the destruction of morality are straight out of "The Communist Manifesto!"

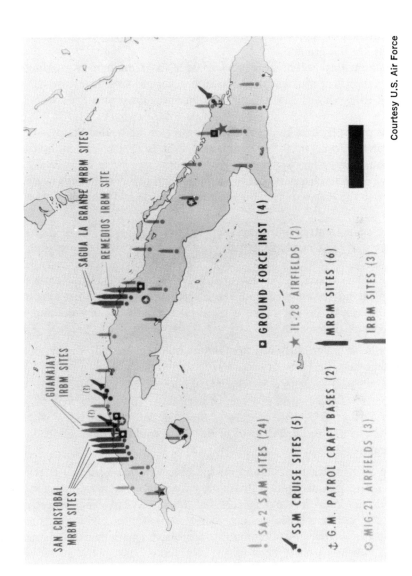

Courtesy U.S. Air Force

SOVIET MILITARY BUILDUP IN CUBA

SAN CRISTOBAL MRBM SITES

GUANAJAY IRBM SITES

SAGUA LA GRANDE MRBM SITES

REMEDIOS IRBM SITE

SA-2 SAM SITES (24)

SSM CRUISE SITES (5)

G.M. PATROL CRAFT BASES (2)

MIG-21 AIRFIELDS (3)

GROUND FORCE INST (4)

IL-28 AIRFIELDS (2)

MRBM SITES (6)

IRBM SITES (3)

21

STEP 6

The next step is that of intimidation. Having softened up a target nation by one or all of the preceding steps, the next move is that of making threats of reprisal or invasion if ever-widening concessions or coalitions are not granted.

In these days of nuclear power, with the Communists holding massive supplies of missiles, not to mention ever-growing naval strength to match its hordes of land troops, this intimidation step is a powerful weapon.

It is presently held in check by the power of the United States, but this deterrent force must be maintained if it is to bar raw military aggression.

As President Nixon said in his 1970 foreign policy statement (with reference to the Russian invasion of Czechoslovakia and the Sino-Soviet clashes),

"we cannot entrust our future entirely to the self-restraint of countries that have not hesitated to use their power even against their allies.

"The quantitative and qualitative improvement of Russia's nuclear might, coupled with the emergence of Communist China as an atomic power, make it essential that this country maintain a posture of strength."

Commenting on this need to maintain military strength, the Washington Star said, on February 22, 1970:

"The President's 'irreducible minimum of essential military security' is the central problem of our times. If we fail to maintain the power to defend ourselves, the state of our relations with Uruguay and the social needs of our cities could become suddenly, permanently and equally irrelevant."

We all know of the Russian missile base in Cuba—held in check only by a direct confrontation by military force of awesome dimension. But we do not know how extensively that threat may have been secretly increased since the classic military confrontation. In any event, the simple truth is that the Communist aggressive encirclement of the United States has already been partly achieved.

STEP 7

"Gain the confidence of the people," says this step. "Study their problems, provide help for them, sell yourself as their friend in aiding them to achieve their goals."

Such were the old siren slogans which beguiled the Russians with "Bread, Peace and Freedom" as their Provisional Government went down to Communist death, and the "agrarian reforms" which hoodwinked the Chinese and the Cubans.

In this fashion, the Communists gain the people's support, or at least avoid their participation in active defense when the Communists make their final move to conquer.

STEP 8

This is subversion. It explains how Lenin with 17 supporters took over Russia's 175,000,000 people with the aid of only 40,000 followers.

Subversion has a thousand faces. It permeates every crack and crevice. It destroys men's spiritual force, it robs them of their standards and principles, it stupifies them with alcohol and drugs, it encourages every vice and sin—and it renders them easy marks for betrayals and well-nigh helpless as defenders of their freedoms. Already slaves to drugs, sex, gambling, treachery, and fearful of riots, turmoils and threats—the defenders of freedom are virtually helpless when the "Trojan Horse" suddenly bursts open and reveals the Communist enemy in their midst.

STEP 9

This is the end. It is voluntary surrender to Communism and the loss of all freedoms.

STEPS AFTER THE TAKE-OVER

STEP 1

Fulfill all promises made in gaining the people's confidence. (Step 6 explains this further.)

STEP 2

Disarm everyone, and confiscate all weapons. At the same time activate a powerful secret police system.

The secret police, as in Latvia for example, "recruited youth to report on their friends and schoolmates. As a result, the feeling of terror and fear crept into family life and mistrust became part of daily life, since those who informed on their fellow citizens were promised rewards and at times threatened with exposure. - - - Communists, after

23

taking over a country, use ruthless terror against those who can stand in their way or lead resistance, in order to paralyze the human mind and make the citizens subservient to Communist rule." (United States Senate Report, 89th Congress, 2nd Session.)

STEP 3

Shoot all of the leaders of the conquered country, and all potential leaders.

(This is where the duped intellectual "leaders" who were used during the preliminary attack period receive their reward.)

High on the list of those who are always eliminated in this critical step because of their qualities of leadership and their numerous followers are labor leaders, Freemasons, and prominent Roman Catholics.

Freemasons have always been found in the forefront of the battle for men's dignity and freedom. In this connection might be recalled such Masonic freedom fighters as Voltaire, Rousseau and Mirabeau of France; the patriot and Mason Simon Bolivar, honored as the liberator of South America; the colorful and ever-remembered Masonic leader Guiseppe Garibaldi who led Italy to freedom in 1870 and Guiseppe Verdi, Grand Master of Masons in Italy who did so much to perpetuate that freedom in modern Italy.

This same history and tradition of devotion to the cause of men's freedoms has, of course, continued in the United States of America. Twenty-three of the thirty-nine signers of the Constitution of the United States, almost sixty percent, were Freemasons. These included such men as George Washington, Alexander Hamilton and Robert Morris. And the example which they set has been followed down through the history of our country to this very day.

STEP 4

Take over all communications and transportation systems.

STEP 5

Set up the new government as the only employer or source of jobs. Everyone will be forced to work where the government dictates, doing what the government dictates and receiving for wages only what the government dictates. No individual will have any choice in the matter.

STEP 6

Take back anything given to the people in Step 1. This was always the plan, and it can now be done safely.

STEP 7

Set up a forced internal spy system—with everyone spying on everyone else, and reporting to the secret police. This is often achieved, as indicated in Step 2.

STEP 8

Register everyone. Forbid all travel outside of a small area—such as a ten mile circle. This will make virtually impossible any effective resistance or the organization of any opposition group.

The "glorious" Communist State is now in full operating condition. You have seen its methods face to face. And you have seen it destroy every freedom.

It is any wonder that freedom-loving people all over the world, including the United States of America, have a common cause against the Communist dictatorship? Would *you* like to live under the doctrines, beliefs and practices of its rule?

Indeed, let us all look at the irrefutable proof of the hatred against Communism of all who experience its rule. That proof stands in the 3,600,000 people who left their homes in East Germany to escape Communism, the approximate 3,000,000 more who moved from China for the same reason, the 2,000,000 who escaped from North Korea to South Korea, and the more than 1,200,000 from European satellites who fled their homelands while they could. That is a total of just under 10,000,000 men, women and children who proved the tyranny of Communism by leaving it when they could.

But there are no instances where significant numbers of people safely in the free world ever reentered a Communist nation.

There is a vote for freedom which no Communist nor Communist sympathizer can answer. If Communism is not the vicious, hated dictator, but the benevolent friend of the people, why do people everywhere leave it by the millions but never make mass migrations back to it?

Courtesy U.S. Air Force

THE BERLIN WALL
Once Conquered—No Escape

HOW IS FREEDOM TO BE DEFENDED AGAINST THIS ENEMY OF INDIVIDUAL DIGNITY AND FREEDOM?

Communism can be halted in its quest for world domination. To achieve that end takes both national and individual action.

First, the lessons of relatively recent history must be learned and applied by every freedom-loving nation, supported by its citizens whom it seeks to protect.

Again, General Lemnitzer gives us the facts. He calls attention to the astounding fact that "During the period 1945-1948, almost 90 million non-Russian peoples and 390,000 square miles of territory fell within the sphere of Soviet influence." He then goes on to describe the purely defensive military alliance (known as NATO) formed in 1949 "- - - to safeguard the freedom, common heritage, and civilization of their peoples, founded on the principles of democracy, individual liberty, and the rule of law."

Then the General puts the critical question. "- - - as to the fear of invasion or subversion, after twenty years of NATO, what have been the results?"

The answer to that question, and the conclusive answer to our inquiry as to how to halt the Communist march to world domination is then given us.

"The simple facts are that NATO Europe has experienced twenty years of peace. - - - During that period not one square inch of NATO territory has been lost to Communist aggression. A generation has grown to maturity in NATO Europe without knowing the horror or chaos of degradation that comes from war."

As the General says, and as our President confirms, there must, then, be adequate defensive military power and preparation to stay the military threats and attacks of Communism.

But much more than this can be done by individuals.

Every American, and especially every young American, should know about the Communist dictatorship and its avowed aim to destroy our country as well as to conquer the rest of the world. We should all remember ex-Premier Khrushchev's vicious threat as he screamed,

27

"Whether you like it or not, history is on our side. We will bury you!"
And we should all remember the words of Lenin, as they have been
printed here.

MEDIUM RANGE
BALLISTIC MISSILE BASE IN CUBA

Next, we must transmit this basic knowledge to our friends and
neighbors.

Having done that, we must use our personal efforts to oppose every
attempt to weaken our people and render them less able to defend their
faith and freedoms. We must insist upon the duty of all citizens to obey
the laws of our Country, lest anarchy and chaos ensue. We must deny
that Man is but a material object, devoid of spirituality, and the helpless
product of his environment. Generations of pioneering Americans who
created this tremendous nation of ours have proved that to be the big
lie. And similar generations of strong Americans have proudly drawn
their strength from God and have followed His mighty commandments
in building our Country. They have proved by their personal experi-

ences that Man can achieve his high destiny. They have overcome their environment, they have created our national heritage, and they have been ever ready to fight for the dignity of Man and for his faith and freedoms.

The individual ownership of property is the very heart of the system of free enterprise upon which our country has built the richest and soundest economy in all history. In this economy the individual is rewarded for his energy, his ingenuity and his thrift. Those qualities are by no means characteristic solely of Americans. They are the endowment of free people everywhere and have made possible the spirit of competition which has been fundamental to progress since life of any kind began to earth.

Ownership of property came as one kind of recognition for the degree and quality of effort expended. It has not only been a firm contribution to our own country's highest standard of living of any nation; it is the backbone of the self-reliance, the independence, and the sense of responsibility which has elevated not only the material but also the spiritual status of the citizens of the United States.

As has been said, energy, ingenuity and thrift characterize peoples other than the American people, but these qualities have been especially strengthened in the course of this nation's history by example, by experience and by precept. They are instilled and encouraged from childhood. In the woodland clearings of the pioneers who conquered a wilderness, all of those qualities were a stern necessity for existence itself; in the homely axioms of the early American philosophers, their importance was hammered home. "Plow deep while sluggards sleep; you will have corn to sell and some to keep"; "A penny saved is a penny earned"; were not buried in the back pages of Poor Richard's Almanac. These were repeated around the nation's firesides and handed down from one generation to the next as a stimulus to earnest effort. As a consequence, every American youth today can look forward to possession of something that is his very own, in which he can take pride and by reason of which he can feel secure.

Opportunities to gain economic independence and security abound in free America. They exist and are employed from the early years of life. Men of ambition, talent and determination have turned a hand to them when, where and whatever they offered. American history is full of examples of those who reached great success from humble beginnings, as a result of their own initiative and willingness to work on the job at hand. Many a distinguished American first traveled the road to greatness on a newspaper delivery route.

And the great majority of Americans still stand for these freedoms and opportunities.

Let these Americans see you, as an individual, responding to the call to act like a responsible free person, and you may be sure that you will not fight alone.

Thus, we can combat the wave of atheism which assails us. We can rebuild the basic moral values upon which our Country was

Courtesy U.S. Air Force

SOVIET MISSILES
EN ROUTE TO CUBA

founded. We can silence the false doctrine that Man is a slave of his environment by the proud history of how our ancestors prevailed over a hostile wilderness to build America. And we can drive the arrogant "master race" intellectual to his knees before the dignity of Man, the immortal spiritual which is within him, and the majesty of God, our Father.

What has been said in this brief description of the Communist dictatorship is no fanciful picture. As Sovereign Grand Commander Henry C. Clausen has previously warned—

"Political tyranny is evidenced most markedly in the world today through International Communism. Make no mistake about the reality

30

of its evil designs. It is rooted in a Karl Marx credo: - - - "forcible overthrow of all existing social conditions" - - - "abolition of all private property," of "eternal truths," and of "all religion and all morality." Its tools are the terrorist contemplation: "famine, pestilence and war. Death for those who oppose Communism and death for our priceless freedoms." The recent pitiful pleas of Czechoslovakia still ring in our ears. Worldwide manipulations issue daily from Moscow to activate revolutionary schemes. Examples are their military supplies to our enemies in North Vietnam, North Korea and Cuba to kill or maim our military men, and their penetration of violence into the free world."

It seems fitting to conclude this message to all free peoples everywhere with the following words of Edward Everett Hale, former Chaplain of the United States Senate:

> I am only one,
> But still I am one.
> I cannot do everything,
> But still I can do something;
> And because I cannot do everything
> I will not refuse to do the
> something that I can do.

YOU CAN HELP TO COMBAT COMMUNISM

Use these weapons

1 INFORMATION
Keep well abreast of current affairs!

2 DEMOCRACY
Take an interest in our government . . . use your vote!

3 ALERTNESS
Recognize propaganda Do not support Communist causes!

SEPARATION
OF
CHURCH
AND
STATE

Edited by

ROBERT B. WATTS, 33°, G∴C∴
Director of Education

TABLE OF CONTENTS

"KEEP THEM SEPARATE"

4

FOREWORD

This is the third volume in our Supreme Council's New Series of **DYNAMIC FREEDOMS**. It is authoritative, accurate and up-to-the-minute. It deals with our priceless American heritage—religious freedom.

The very heart of our constitutional freedoms is religious liberty. We bolted and riveted down the ecumenical concept long before the word became popular. And it is only in such a climate as ours that all religions can live and grow.

The constitutional right to insist on church-state separation is ours. We should not let it be trampled upon or thrown into the junkyard. It represents values for which men died. This right does not exist in many places of the world. It is our unique national heritage and needs constant rediscovery and protection if we are not going to fade into political oblivion.

This booklet will give you the facts, and make clear the perils to our religious freedom that exist today. It will tell you in simple language how every religion is in danger unless we insist that the State stay out of the affairs of the Church and that the Church stay out of the affairs of the State. "Good fences make good neighbors."

Truly, this booklet is most timely since we are faced today with one of the "three great perils" that Washington foresaw "will come upon the Republic." That third peril includes the possibility we may be led to deviate from our time-tested, paramount, Constitutional safeguards of American freedoms. It behooves each of us to do what we can to protect that great heritage.

For a program of vigilant action and personal participation, may I suggest:

    1. *Stand up and speak out.* Make your voice heard. Coura-

geously tell the American story. Become a mighty champion of freedom for all freedom-loving people.

2. *Pound home the lessons of history.* Consider, if you will, the letter, the spirit and the purpose of our Constitution in light of the warnings of history. Our early settlers were moved to seek refuge on our shores from spiritual despotism. Let's help make their vision a continuing reality.

Sovereign Grand Commander

GUIDELINES FOR CHURCH-STATE RELATIONS

UNITED STATES CONSTITUTION:
FIRST AMENDMENT

"Congress shall make no law respecting an establishment of religion, or prohibiting the free exercise thereof . . ."

UNITED STATES CONSTITUTION:
FOURTEENTH AMENDMENT

"No State shall make or enforce any law which shall abridge the privileges or immunities of citizens of the United States; . . ."

THOMAS JEFFERSON:

". . . to compel a man to furnish contributions of money for the propagation of opinions he disbelieves and abhors, is sinful and tyrannical . . ."

The 1779 Virginia Bill for
Establishing Religious Freedom

THOMAS JEFFERSON:

"I consider the Government of the United States as interdicted by the Constitution from intermeddling with religious institutions, their doctrines, disciplines or exercises. Civil powers alone have been given to the President of the United States."

BENJAMIN FRANKLIN:

"When a religion is good, I conceive it will support itself; and when it does not support itself, and God does not take care to support it so that its professors are obliged to call for help of the civil power, 'tis a sign, I apprehend, of its being a bad one."

DAVID DUDLEY FIELD:

"The greatest achievement ever made in the cause of human progress is the total and final separation of Church and State. If we had nothing else to boast of, we could lay claim with justice that first among the nations we of this country made it an article of organic law that the relations between man and his Maker were a private concern, into which other men have no right to intrude. To measure the stride thus made for the Emancipation of the race, we have only to look back over the centuries that have gone before us, and recall the dreadful persecutions in the name of religion that have filied the world.

Church and State in the United States
by Anson Phelps Stokes

GEORGE WASHINGTON:

"The Government of the United States of America is not in any sense founded on the Christian Religion."

ULYSSES S. GRANT:

"Encourage free schools, and resolve that not one dollar of money shall be appropriated to the support of any sectarian school. Resolve that neither the state nor nation, or both combined, shall support institutions of learning other than those sufficient to afford every child growing up in the land the opportunity of a good common school education, unmixed with sectarian . . . tenets. Leave the matter of religion to the family, the altar, the church and the private schools, supported by private contributions. Keep the church and the state forever separated."

Speaking in Des Moines, Iowa
1875

JOHN F. KENNEDY:

"I believe in an America where the separation of church and state is absolute—where no Catholic prelate would tell the President (should he be a Catholic) how to act, and no Protestant minister would tell his parishioners for whom to vote—where no church or church school is granted any public funds or political preference. . . ."

Speaking at Houston, Texas
September 12, 1960

JOHN F. KENNEDY:

"There can be no question of federal funds being used for support of parochial or private schools. It's unconstitutional under the First Amendment as interpreted by the Supreme Court. I'm opposed to the Federal Government's extending support to any church or its schools."

Look Magazine, March 3, 1959

GUIDELINES

ABRAHAM LINCOLN:

"The United States Government must not undertake to run the churches. When an individual in a church, or out of it, becomes dangerous to the public interest, he must be checked."

JAMES CONNOLLY:

"Whenever the clergy succeeded in conquering political power in any country the result has been disastrous to the interests of religion and inimical to the progress of humanity."

UNITED STATES SUPREME COURT:

"The 'establishment of religion' clause of the First Amendment means at least this: Neither a state nor the Federal Government can set up a church. Neither can pass laws which aid one religion, aid all religions, or prefer one religion over another. . . No tax in any amount, large or small, can be levied to support any religious activities or institutions, whatever they may be called, or whatever form they may adopt to teach or practice religion. Neither a state nor the Federal Government can, openly or secretly, participate in the affairs of any religious organizations or groups and vice versa. In the words of Jefferson, the clause against establishment of religion by law was intended to erect 'a wall of separation between Church and State'."

> *Everson* v. *Board of Education,*
> 330 U.S. 1 (1947)
> *McCollum* v. *Board of Education of*
> *Champaign, Ill.* 333 U.S. 203 (1948)
> *Torcaso* v. *Watkins,* 367 U.S. 488
> (1961)

JUSTICE HUGO L. BLACK:

"When the power, prestige and financial support of government is placed behind a particular religious belief, the indirect coercive pressure upon religious minorities to conform to the prevailing officially approved religion is plain . . .

"The same history showed that many people lost their respect for any religion that had relied upon the support of government to spread its faith."

> *Engel* v. *Vitale,* 370 U.S. 421
> (1962)

9

GUIDELINES

JUSTICE TOM C. CLARK:

"It is no defense to urge that the religious practices here may be relatively minor encroachments on the First Amendment. The breach of neutrality that is today a trickling stream may all too soon become a raging torrent; and in the words of Madison, 'It is proper to take alarm at the first experiment on our liberties.' "

Abington School District v. *Schempp*
374 U.S. 203 (1963)

JUSTICE ROBERT H. JACKSON:

"Catholic education is the rock on which the whole structure rests, and to render tax aid to its Church School is indistinguishable to me from rendering the same aid to the Church itself."

Dissident in *Everson* v. *Board of Education,* 330 U.S. 1, 24 (1947)

JUSTICE WILEY RUTLEDGE:

"Public money devoted to payment of religious cost, educational or other, brings the quest for more. It brings, too, the struggle of sect against sect for the larger share or for any. . . That is precisely the history of societies which have had an established religion and dissident groups. It is the very thing Jefferson and Madison experienced and sought to guard against, whether in its blunt or in its more screened forms. The end of such strife cannot be other than to destroy the cherished liberty. . ."

Everson v. *Board of Education* (above)

HENRY CLAY:

"All religions united with government are more or less inimical to liberty. All separated from government are compatible with liberty."

ANDREW JACKSON:

"I could not do otherwise without transcending the limits prescribed by the Constitution for the President; and without feeling that I might in some degree disturb the security which religion nowadays enjoys in this country in its complete separation from the political concerns of the General Government."

Statement: Refusing to proclaim a national fast day of prayers.

GUIDELINES

JAMES KNOX POLK:

"Thank God, under our Constitution there was no connection between Church and State; and that in my action as President of the United States I recognized no distinction of creeds in my appointments to office."

FELIX FRANKFURTER:

"The great leaders of the American Revolution were determined to remove political support from every religious establishment. . ."

Dissent: *W. Va. Board of Education*
v. *Barnette,* 319 U.S. 653
(1943)

SAMUEL T. SPEAK:

"Masterly inactivity on the part of the State, in the sense of leaving the maintenance, propagation, and administration of the Christian religion entirely to the voluntary principle, is just the position to call forth the intensest activity on the part of the Church. It is the best position for the State to derive from both the largest quantity of moral power which is possible to apply in this imperfect world."

Religion and the State

JUSTICE HUGO BLACK:

"The First Amendment has erected a wall between church and state. That wall must be kept high and impregnable. We could not approve the slightest breach."

Majority Opinion: *Everson* v. *Board of Education,* 330 U.S. 1
(1947)

EUGENE CARSON BLAKE:

"Twice in the last 12 months, I have been in Communist Europe. It is quite clear to me, as it was not before I went, that one of the reasons for what popular support remains for the Communist governments is the people's satisfaction that at least one good thing was accomplished—that the wealth and political domination of the church has been broken."

Writing in *The Churchman,* Dec. 1, 1956

11

CHAPTER I

HISTORY OF
CHURCH-STATE RELATIONS

THE AMERICAN ARRANGEMENT

The American plan of separation between church and state is something unique. It is to this day not at all the rule among the nations, but rather the glittering exception. Separation is new. Union of church and state with governmental sponsorship and subsidy of religion is old. Indeed, the latter was all the world knew up until 200 years ago. While the idea is gaining, it can still be said that nations which have discovered and embraced the separation principle are comparatively few.

A GLANCE AT THE PAST

One has only to look across the pages of history to realize how completely the union of church and state has dominated the past. We read in the Book of Genesis that "Joseph made it a law over the land of Egypt . . . that Pharaoh should have the fifth part, except the land of the priests only. . ." This meant that whereas the Pharaoh exacted a tax of 20 percent upon all land, that owned by the clergy was exempt. Not only that, Pharaoh himself paid them tribute and they enjoyed great ecclesiastical estates worked by armies of slaves. It is estimated that the priests owned 750,000 acres in the fertile Nile valley—about 15 percent of the total and that, all told, they enjoyed about one-third of the national income.

In both Persia and India the unfortunate intrusion of state upon church and church upon state resulted in all manner of suffering. Persia saw the two-edged sword of oppression wielded by priest and king. In India, a conquering army perpetuated its power by a system of religious beliefs and practices. But in the Western World we find perhaps the most convincing demonstration of the evil and folly of their union. In A.D. 325 the Roman Emperor Constantine brought church and state into an alliance which proved to be disastrous for both. Church and clergy were given preferred status and rich subsidies from the state and the provision that only its members could hold public office. The wealth of all who died intestate or without direct heirs was automatically bestowed upon the church. Churches were repaired and erected with public funds. The institutions of the church were generously subsidized by government, while the clergy drew generous emoluments for their administration of the sacraments. Furthermore, the state undertook to extirpate what the church called false religion and incorrect doctrine. Pagan worship was proscribed and pagan temples were razed. An even harsher fate was meted out to deviationist forms of Christianity. Persons holding such differing views were liquidated as "haters of Christ and enemies of truth and life, in league with the devil and destruction."

The Reformation, which was political and economic as well as religious, began a process of change. But to preserve the gains that were made for freedom required the agony of the Thirty Years War. In that conflict more than 15 million persons perished by violence. It took Germany 200 years to recover the population it lost through this war. How hardly was freedom won!

REVOLUTIONS OF MANKIND

It is well known that the pages of history are red with the blood of religious wars generated in the hostile claims of church and church or church and state. The Great Armada which sailed for Britain in 1583 was bound on a mission to conquer the heretics and restore the "true faith" in that country. The Spanish ships were well stocked with instruments of torture designed to wring confessions from the heretics and persuade them to embrace "the true religion." The French Revolution in the 18th century and the English Revolution two centuries earlier were deeply concerned with the church-state issue. One of the besetting national causes was the church holdings of vast tax-exempt lands and the clerical enjoyment of huge tax-exempt incomes. The revolutions were violent corrective measures.

Mexico was another country where an over-abundance of church institutionalism brought the country to revolution. It is within the memory of persons now living to recall the fury of the movement which resulted in the complete confiscation of church property. To this day the church in Mexico may not now even own its own houses of worship. These belong to the state. Church control of education was broken

14

and even seminaries for the training of clergy were forbidden. It is against the law in Mexico for a clergyman to appear on the street clad in his clerical garb. Such extreme measures are the logical outcome of a church-state union where the church was given preferred treatment and obtains an inordinate amount of the nation's property and wealth.

When the United States intervened in The Philippines just before the turn of the century, the big problem was not the Spanish government but rather the church which had managed to gain possession of 400,000 acres of the best land. The United States did not expropriate the church. Instead, it paid $7½ million in gold for 300,000 acres. This land was then redistributed among the populace. Also, we established a system of public schools designed to break the church's monopoly on education.

Thus, in one revolution after another the problem is seen to be that of church-state relations. Abuses have had their consequence in war, persecution, and expropriation.

PROFOUND CHANGES

Looking back over the course of church-state relations in the West, one can observe two profound changes. First, the change in the fourth century when Christians ceased to be a sect of those who voluntarily joined and became, instead, a group coterminous with the citizenship of the Empire. Second, the profound change when the American Founding Fathers restored religion to its voluntary status.

CHAPTER II

HOW CHURCH-STATE SEPARATION CAME ABOUT

ARCHITECTS OF SEPARATION

The architects of church-state separation were for the most part men of religion. Sectarian leaders in the 17th and 18th centuries were leading advocates. They had suffered so much at the hands of both Roman Catholic and Protestant establishments of religion that they dreamed of separation of church and state as an ideal solution to their problems. As early as 1614 a Baptist leader, Leonard Busher, addressed a petition to King James I:

> Kings and magistrates are to rule temporal affairs by the swords of their temporal kingdoms, and bishops and ministers are to rule spiritual affairs by the Word and Spirit of God, the sword of Christ's spiritual kingdom, and not to intermeddle with one another's authority, office and function.

Roger Williams, a Baptist minister, was an early American exponent of church-state separation. Williams argued in his *Bloudy Tenent* that religious persecution is wrong because "it confounds the civil and religious" and because "States . . . are proved essentially civil."

Isaac Backus, a Baptist pastor, had great influence in the struggle for separation in the Colonies. In 1775 he inspired and probably wrote a letter from the Warren Baptist Association protesting certain features of the Congregational establishment in Massachusetts. In it appear these words:

> We are persuaded that an entire freedom from being taxed by civil rulers to religious worship, is not a mere favor from any man or men in the world, but a right and property granted us by God, who commands us to stand fast in it. . .

Backus appeared before the Constitutional Convention in 1787 to plead for a provision guaranteeing religious liberty and freedom from the tax for religion.

16

Another Baptist pastor who exerted great influence for religious liberty was John Leland of Virginia. He frequently appeared before the Virginia Assembly as a spokesman for this cause. His particular goal was disestablishment of the Episcopal Church in Virginia. Leland was deeply worried when the United States Constitution was up for ratification without strong religious liberty guarantees. He was a candidate against James Madison. But after listening to Madison's argument for immediate ratification and his assurance that an amendment providing for church-state separation would be promptly forthcoming, Leland withdrew and threw the election to his opponent. Madison made good on his commitment and the First Amendment with its guarantees of basic liberties was the result. John Leland was a great friend of both Jefferson and Madison and undoubtedly exerted a considerable influence on both.

John Witherspoon, a Presbyterian minister, Signer of the Declaration of Independence, whose statue stands on Connecticut Avenue in Washington, D. C., was a consistent advocate of religious liberty. He constantly stressed that mere toleration was inadequate since this indicated only superiority and condescension. He contended that complete religious liberty to worship how one chose, or not at all, was the only proper plan for a republic, and also that every church should be supported by donations of its own members without recourse to the taxing power of the state.

It is interesting that Witherspoon refused to interpret separation of church and state as barring clergymen from running for public office. Some had taken this position and such a ban had even been placed in certain state constitutions, but Witherspoon insisted that this was an infringement upon liberty.

MADISON AND JEFFERSON

James Madison and Thomas Jefferson, both of whom became President, both Virginians, are properly known as the architects of our American plan of separation of church and state. Madison was aroused to protest by the laws which established the Anglican Church in Virginia and made life difficult for dissenters. Eventually, these laws were relaxed and a move was on foot to change from an exclusive Anglican establishment to one which would provide taxes for several leading denominations. Madison's *Memorial and Remonstrance Against Religious Assessments* not only provided a crushing indictment of the proposed establishment but gave mankind one of the finest statements of religious liberty ever penned. Certainly the *Remonstrance* and Jefferson's Bill for Establishing Religious Freedom did more than anything else, save possibly the debates on the First Amendment itself, to set the tone of friendly church-state separation in the United States.

Madison's flashing insights illumined the church-state debate in Virginia and set the stage for the First Amendment. In attacking Patrick Henry's religious assessment bill, Madison insisted that the point was "not is Religion necessary—but are Religious Establishments necessary for Religion?" He insisted that religion was corrupted when established by law and that religious establishments contributed to the downfall of states. It was Madison's masterly strategy as much as anything else that defeated the religious assessment bill and paved the way for separation of church and state in the Commonwealth of Virginia.

Thomas Jefferson, author of the Declaration of Independence and the Bill for Establishing Religious Freedom in Virginia, and our third President, was a devout believer in the separation of church and state. The bill provided:

> That no man shall be compelled to frequent or support any religious worship, place, or ministry whatsoever, nor shall be enforced, restrained, molested or burthened in his body or goods, nor shall otherwise suffer, on account of his religious opinions or belief; but that all men shall be free to profess, and by argument to maintain, their opinions in matters of religion, and that the same shall in no wise diminish, enlarge, or effect their civil capacities.

Jefferson himself placed this bill, along with his authorship of the Declaration of Independence and his founding of the University of Virginia, as the three significant achievements of his life. Ever friendly to the cause of religion but quick to denounce any governmental intervention in this area, Jefferson was a consistent advocate of complete church-state separation.

THE SHAPE OF CHURCH-STATE SEPARATION

It was that wise observer, James Bryce, who detected and pointed out the greatest single factor in America's political success. He wrote in his *American Commonwealth:*

> "Half the wars of Europe, half the internal troubles that have vexed the European states . . . have arisen from

the rival claims of church and state. This whole vast chapter of debate and strife has remained virtually unopened in the United States."

What was the secret of avoiding this strife of state against church and church against church? The concept of separation of church and state. The inter-functioning of the two was bad. And why? Because this mingled the coercive processes of government with the free, voluntary operations of religion. A coerced religion is not a religion. To be authentic, religion must take its rise from the free conscience of the individual. This explains why a religion with state sponsorship and patronage usually ends up as a dead formalism without support or love among the people.

CHAPTER III

WHAT SEPARATION MEANT

Our Founding Fathers saw all that Lord Bryce saw. They were determined to avoid in the New World the kind of church-state strife that had cursed and crippled the Old. They resolved, insofar as relations with the state were concerned, to restore religion to the status it had enjoyed as a free, voluntary society in the fourth century. They wrote the First Amendment:

Congress shall make no law respecting an establishment of religion or prohibiting the free exercise thereof; . .

"No law" meant no law. Government was to be neutral among religious groups, neither inhibiting nor promoting. Not only was there to be "no establishment" of religion, there was to be nothing about this, nothing which pertained to this. The no-establishment clause meant that Government was to keep its hands off the churches and its nose out of religion. "Masterly inactivity" was to be the Government stance in regard to religion. Again, let us say that this idea was sensationally new. It was also devastatingly simple. If the amalgam of state and church which had persisted for centuries had been manifestly evil in its effects, why not replace it? Why not, indeed, restore religion to the free, voluntary role it had enjoyed in the real heyday of its strength? This was the logic of the Founding Fathers as they drew up the First Amendment which separated church and state in the United States.

Henceforth the state would not shore up religion or promote it in any sense. The churches would be free to produce whatever they were capable of producing. Religion would be eminently a private affair, taking its rise from the free choice and free desire of the people. Churches would be composed, not of citizens, but of members who voluntarily joined their congregations.

ABOVE ALL—MONEY

As the debates on the First Amendment make abundantly clear, the Founders were much concerned with the financing of religion. This, too, they insisted must be voluntary. To tax people for religion was a contradiction in terms. It was to coerce what from its very essence must be free. So James Madison wrote in his famed *Memorial and Remonstrance:*

> Who does not see . . . that the same authority which can force a citizen to contribute three pence only of his property for the support of any one establishment, may force him to conform to any other establishment, in all cases whatsoever?

In his Bill for Establishing Religious Freedom, Thomas Jefferson declared

> "that to compel a man to furnish contributions of money for the propagation of opinions which he disbelieves, is sinful and tyrannical."

THE COLONIAL ESTABLISHMENTS

There were, to be sure, establishments of religion in nine of the Thirteen Colonies, and taxes were levied to support them. There was nothing in the First Amendment to ban such establishments since the inhibition there applied only to Congress. Actually, state establishments of religion persisted until Massachusetts terminated its Congregational establishment in 1833. But with the passage of the Fourteenth Amendment, the Federal prohibition also became a state impairment of the establishment, and free exercise clauses became a fact. The Fourteenth Amendment states:

> No State shall make or enforce any law which shall abridge the privileges or immunities of citizens of the United States; . . .

This meant that state governments, like the Federal Government, could not pass laws respecting establishment of religion. It should be noted, too, that every state admitted to the Union since 1876 was required by Congress to write into its constitution a provision that it maintain a public school system "free of sectarian control."

It is frequently said that the First Amendment erected a "wall of separation" between church and state. This expression originated with Thomas Jefferson, third President of the United States, and one of the Founding Fathers. In a carefully worded letter to the Danbury Baptist Association he wrote:

> I contemplate with sovereign reverence that act of the whole American people which declared that their legislature

21

should "make no law respecting an establishment of religion, or prohibiting the free exercise thereof," thus building a wall of separation between church and state.

The expression "wall of separation" has been used repeatedly by the Supreme Court in defining church-state relations.

At least two other Presidents of the United States have spoken out with especial clarity on the separation of church and state. President Ulysses S. Grant, speaking in 1875 in Des Moines, Iowa declared:

> Encourage free schools, and resolve that not one dollar of money shall be appropriated to the support of any sectarian school. Resolve that neither the state nor the nation, or both combined, shall support institutions of learning other than those sufficient to afford every child growing up in the land the opportunity of a good common school education, unmixed with sectarian . . . tenets. Leave the matter of religion to the family, the altar, the church, and the private school, supported entirely by private contributions. Keep the church and state forever separate.

Just prior to his election, President John F. Kennedy said, September 12, 1960, in Houston, Texas:

> I believe in an America where the separation of church and state is absolute—where no Catholic prelate would tell the President (should he be a Catholic) how to act, and no Protestant minister would tell his parishioners for whom to vote—where no church or church school is granted any public funds or political preference . . .

And on March 3, 1959, as a Presidential candidate, Senator Kennedy said:

> There can be no question of federal funds being used for support of parochial or private schools. It's unconstitutional under the First Amendment as interpreted by the Supreme Court. I'm opposed to the federal government's extending support to any church or its schools.

BEWARE THAT NICE WIDE ROAD

CHAPTER IV

SEPARATION AND RELIGION

FRIENDLY SEPARATION

In making a definite break with state-supported, state-sponsored religion, the Founding Fathers were in no sense hostile to religion itself. They were taking government out of the business of religion, not to hurt religion but to help it. They wanted to give it free opportunity. Justice Welch of the Supreme Court of Ohio caught the spirit of separation in his opinion in *Cincinnati Board of Education* v. *Minor.* He said:

> Government is an organization for particular purposes. It is not almighty, and we are not to look to it for everything. The great bulk of human affairs and human interests is left by any free government to individual enterprise and individual action. Religion is eminently one of these interests, lying outside the true and legitimate province of government. (See Samuel T. Speak, *Religion and the State,* New York, Dodd Mead & Co., 1876 p. 130.)

It should not be forgotten that separation of church and state in the United States was effected by men who were friendly to religion. They were not attempting to use separation as a device to hamper and stunt the religious forces of the Colonies. Just the opposite. The termination of the various church establishments was in no sense prompted by "anti-clericalism." The very term has been practically unknown in America. There has never been in the United States, as yet, a domination of political affairs by a church such as would provoke anti-clericalism.

The friendliness of the rule of separation toward the churches is underscored by the fact that among the chief proponents of the principle were churchmen. The Baptists, as already noted, were all out for separation. They not only passed resolutions but organized and

24

did the leg work necessary to get the idea embodied in laws and constitutions. John Leland, a Baptist leader, wrote in 1790 that the matter of separating church and state "has been so canvassed for 14 years, and has so far prevailed, that in Virginia, a politician can no more be popular without possession of it, than a preacher who denies the doctrine of the new birth. . ."

The clergymen of the day were in no sense a group of men hanging on to prerequisites and prerogatives from which the people were trying to pry them loose. The Hanover Presbytery in 1778 strongly endorsed church-state separation, explaining its position in these words:

> Neither does the Church of Christ stand in need of a general assessment for its support; and most certain we are persuaded that it would be no advantage, but an injury to the society to which we belong.

The Methodists, as soon as they came into full management of their own affairs, became enthusiastic supporters of church-state separation, and, in time the Congregationalists, Episcopalians, Lutherans, Adventists, Roman Catholics in America and many other groups, no less so. It is close to the mark to say that all religious denominations in the United States came to accept church-state separation gracefully and thankfully.

The friendly basis of church-state separation is demonstrated, again, by the leaders of the time. The men who framed a constitution without a religious establishment and secured its adoption were churchmen, almost without exception. Many of them were devout. George Washington, James Madison, Thomas Jefferson, George Mason, Samuel Livermore, Benjamin Franklin and Charles Pinckney were all Episcopalians. A man like Franklin was, of course, nominal in his churchmanship, yet he generously contributed to various churches and had firm faith in God and prayer. Isaac Backus and John Leland were Baptist preachers; John Witherspoon and Samuel Davies were clergymen of the Presbyterian Church. Actually, Thomas Paine, deist and free-thinker, was about the only non-churchman among them.

When James Madison wrote: "Religion is not within the purview of human government," he was not attacking religion or seeking to penalize it. He was stating what seemed to him an indubitable and significant truth. These churchmen did not hate themselves; they were not trying to cut their own throats. They were not lacking in respect for the institution which had nurtured them. On the contrary, they believed that separation of church and state was a natural and proper arrangement since religion was not within the purview of government. They believed that both church and state would do well when separated.

FRIENDLY V. HOSTILE SEPARATION

The meaning of such friendly separation can only be appreciated as we compare it with hostile separation. The constitutions of the United States and the USSR have sometimes been compared, since both appear to separate church and state. But there is a difference between friendly separation in the United States and hostile separation in the USSR. This difference lies in the second clause of the First Amendment of the United States Constitution which assures the "free exercise" of religion. Congress shall not pass any law respecting an an establishment of religion—"or prohibiting the free exercise thereof." The USSR provision is worth reading:

> In order to insure citizens freedom of conscience, the Church in the USSR is separated from the State, and the school from the Church. Freedom of religious worship and freedom of anti-religious propaganda are recognized for all citizens.

It should be noted that whereas religion is assured of freedom of worship, anti-religion is assured of freedom of propaganda. Churches in Russia may be established by groups desiring them and their right to hold services in them is recognized. What they are forbidden to do is to witness to their faith! It is, for example, a civil offense to teach religion to anyone under the age of 18. No evangelism, no missions, no study groups, no witness. In short, no "free exercise." But it is "free exercise" that it is specifically guaranteed by the United States Constitution. And that free exercise is, in the United States, limited only by general restraints such as are necessary to society's existence and by common sense requirements of decency and health.

IN THE STATES

The authors of the state constitutions undertook to remove any doubt as to the meaning of the First Amendment by drafting "little First Amendments" which spelled out its meaning. Such provisions are now found in virtually all the state constitutions. To offer a typical example, the Illinois Constitution at Article VIII, Section 3, reads as follows:

Neither the General Assembly nor any county, city, town, township, school district, or other public corporation shall ever make any appropriation, or pay from any public fund whatever, anything in aid of any church or sectarian purpose, or to help support or sustain any school, academy, seminary, college, university or other literary or scientific institutions, controlled by any church or sectarian denomination whatever; nor shall any grant or donation of land, money or other personal property ever be made by the State or any public corporation to any church or for any sectarian purpose.

It would be impossible to articulate the point more clearly. What the Founders meant by separation of church and state was that churches and their institutions should be supported by voluntary donations—not by taxes.

CHAPTER V

CHURCH-STATE PROBLEMS

THE FEDERAL POWER

A powerful impact on church-state arrangements has been made by a variety of Federal programs in recent years. Beginning in 1963 there was a program under which church-related institutions of higher learning could receive Federal grants for construction of buildings on their campuses. Many such institutions have survived and have greatly expanded their programs as a result of this aid. In 1965 Congress passed, and the President signed into law, a bill which provides important forms of aid for sectarian elementary and secondary schools. Even before these laws there was the Hill-Burton Act which supplied construction funds for church-related hospitals.

The Economic Opportunity Act of 1964 also involved certain forms of aid for churches in carrying out the purpose of seeking to reduce poverty. Housing programs, urban redevelopment, donation of Goverment surplus—all new phases of Federal activity—sometimes involved church-state relations. Serious questions about church-state relations and even the constitutionality of certain programs were raised.

The effect of the Federal programs on the states was very serious. The language of the establishment clause of the First Amendment was less specific than the state provisions. It had been composed before the public school system had evolved. Under its more general language, Congressional leaders essayed various forms of aid to church schools which they felt would have a chance to squeeze by. All acknowledged that these aids closely skirted the bounds of the permissible if, indeed, they did not trespass beyond them. Nevertheless, being under sectarian pressures, they went ahead, basing their actions on the so-called "child benefit" theory. This was the theory that the aid given was not to the church or to the church school, but only to the students in the school.

CHURCH-STATE PROBLEMS

If the constitutionality of these programs under the First Amendment were dubious, there was scarcely room for doubt at the state level. Virtually all the Federal programs would have been unconstitutional if measured against the state constitutions. This matter became a problem because public school officials in the states were in charge of administering the Federal programs. Thus, these officials were frequently placed in the position of having to administer the very kind of programs which their oath of office forbade! States handled the problem in different ways. Some states forbade the programs; others permitted them with the stipulation that only Federal funds could be used. Missouri had it both ways. The Supreme Court ruled out "shared time" programs for the state but the attorney general ruled that such programs could be pursued, if only federal funds were employed. It seemed apparent that some clarification of constitutionality by the Supreme Court was needed.

RELIGION IN THE SCHOOLS

Another focal point of church-state controversy concerned religious observances in the public schools. One of the arguments originally advanced by Roman Catholic advocates of a separate, sectarian system was that the public schools were "Protestant schools." By this they meant that certain Protestant worship practices were imposed on all students in at least some public schools and that this made these institutions unpalatable to them. The practices to which they objected were steadily eliminated during the early 20th century, and by the 1960's the sole survivor was the practice of Bible reading and prayer in some public schools. All compulsory exercises were ordered from the schools by decision of the Supreme Court in the 1960's. Disappointed sectarians then mounted an effort to amend the First Amendment to permit such practices. The movement seemed to be languishing after an initial burst of interest.

OTHER CHURCH-STATE PROBLEMS

A variety of church-state problems continue to emerge. Baltimore, Maryland had an ordinance which provided that when a church was acquired under condemnation proceedings for some public purpose, such as a freeway, the city must pay the full replacement value. Other property was to be compensated on the basis of "fair value," but churches, and churches alone, received the larger payment. The

Baltimore corporation counsel challenged the statute as an act respecting establishment of religion.

Then there was the matter of transportation and textbooks for church schools. Were these forms of aid to religious education proscribed by the First Amendment and state constitutional provisions? The decision of the United States Court on this matter will be discussed elsewhere. Nearly half the states now have whole or partial support for transportation to parochial schools. Current litigation on the subject is pending in the courts of West Virginia and Minnesota. Delaware is considering a constitutional amendment which would authorize state expenditures for this purpose. State courts have divided on the issue according to the strictness of their church-state provisions. A recent opinion by the Hawaiian Supreme Court in *Honda* v. *Spears* held that bus transportation to religious schools at public expense violated that State's constitution.

Six states now provide textbooks for sectarian schools. State courts also differed on this matter, but the United States Supreme Court has apparently given the green light on this—provided the law is properly drafted to avoid church-state complications.

Urban redevelopment and surplus property donations by the U.S. Department of Health, Education and Welfare have created church-state problems. Is it possible to use the government's condemnation authority to acquire properties to be resold to churches at substantial loss to the taxpayers? What about donations of government surplus real estate and other property to churches for education and welfare programs? What about tax exemption for church property and wholly unrelated business activities, the profits from which run into astronomical figures in many instances—a matter which is increasingly coming under question? What about the preferred status of churches, religious orders and clergy under provisions of the Internal Revenue Code and Regulations?

Sunday laws which prohibit certain kinds of commercial business on that day still apply in some states. In early litigation, courts upheld these laws on the ground that the legislature had authority to protect the Christian day of worship from desecration. But in recent decisions the ground has shifted. Courts have tended to uphold these laws on the ground of health and welfare. It is beneficial to the people to have a prescribed day of rest. The enforced day of rest on Sunday has worked hardships on those whose day of worship falls on a different day. Seventh-day Adventists and Hebrews are examples. The Supreme

Court recently has upheld Sunday laws on the health and welfare ground, but the decision was split. Undoubtedly, this issue will come to the Court again.

"Shared time" between public and parochial schools has been a continuing source of controversy in communities and in the courts. This involves the enrollment of parochial school students in public schools for certain courses of study. Originally, this meant the busing of parochial students to the public schools. More recently, some have shifted the program to bring public school teachers for these subjects into the parochial classrooms. The courts have provided no clear answer to the constitutional problems here. Their findings have been diverse as have the rulings of attorneys general.

CHAPTER VI

CHURCH AND STATE IN THE COURTS

Basically, the problem of the courts has been to strike a balance between no establishment of religion and free exercise of religion. Under our system, government must be neutral in regard to religion. It may not promote nor inhibit religion as this would be something "respecting establishment." On the other hand, government may not lean so far toward "no establishment" of religion that it prevents its free exercise. Under separation of church and state we are entitled to have both and they must be kept in balance.

NO ESTABLISHMENT AND FREE EXERCISE

Let us assume, by way of example, that a lawsuit should be brought by atheists challenging use of public funds for military chaplains Since these men are paid with tax funds and concern themselves with religious matters, the plaintiffs might contend that the whole chaplaincy program was an act respecting establishment of religion and should be terminated as a violation of the First Amendment. But the defense would counter by showing that when men are drafted or go into military service they are separated from the religious opportunities to which they have long been accustomed in their home communities, and that under the "free exercise" clause government has an obligation to make it up to them in some way. So the courts seek a balance between the two provisions of "no establishment" and "free exercise."

A notable "free exercise" case was that of *Torcaso* v. *Watkins* in 1961. Roy Torcaso was appointed a notary public in Maryland but was refused a commission because he would not declare his belief in God. This was legally a requirement for the commission. The Maryland Constitution provided that no religious test shall be required as a qualification for any state office "other than a declaration of belief in the existence of God." The Supreme Court of the United States unanimously held that this requirement was unconstitutional. In his opinion Justice Black held that no government in the United

State can force or influence a person to go to or stay away from a church, or force him to profess a belief or disbelief in any religion; that no person can be punished for professing or entertaining beliefs or disbeliefs; that neither a state nor the Federal Government—

> can constitutionally pass laws or impose requirements which aid all religions as against non-believers, and neither can aid those religions based on beliefs in the existence of God as against those religions founded on different beliefs.

The concern of the courts for the free exercise of religion can be seen nowhere more clearly than in the Mormon polygamy case of the 1870's, and the cases involving religion and the use of drugs in the 1960's and 1970's. Congress had enacted a statute making polygamy a criminal offense. Charged with the offense, the defendant Reynolds pleaded his right to free exercise of religion. He set forth that his church, Latter-day Saints of Jesus Christ, commonly called Mormon, taught that the practice of polygamy was a binding religious obligation. The Supreme Court faced the matter of definition of religion. It did not undertake a formal definition but it did satisfy itself that whatever the word means, the First Amendment does not inhibit government from moving "to reach actions which were in violation of social duties or subversive of good order."

A classic case concerning the free exrcise of religion was that of *Murdock* v. *Commonwealth of Pennsylvania* in 1943. The Supreme Court was confronted with a statute of the City of Jeannette, Pennsylvania which required a license of all persons canvassing or soliciting for orders within the borough limits. Members of the Jehovah's Witnesses who had been carrying on their distribution of literature and solicitation from door to door were haled to court and fined for violating the ordinance.

The Supreme Court held in this case that the ordinance was a violation of the "free exercise" clause of the First Amendment which was made binding on the states through the Fourteenth Amendment. Said the Court: "It could hardly be denied that a tax laid specifically on the exercise of those freedoms would be unconstitutional. Yet the license tax imposed by this ordinance is in substance just that. . ." The Court continued:

> It is one thing to impose a tax on the income or property of a preacher. It is quite another thing to exact a tax from him for the privilege of delivering a sermon. The tax imposed by the City of Jeannette is a flat license tax, the payment of

which is a condition of the exercise of those constitutional privileges. The power to tax the exercise of a privilege is the power to control or suppress its enjoyment.

DRUGS AND FREE EXERCISE

More contemporary cases are those where defendants alleged that the distribution and use of hallucinatory drugs was necessary to the practice of their religion. A famous case in the 1960's involved the Native American Church composed of Indians in our West who were charged with possession and use of peyote, a drug which produces an hallucinatory state. The church's defense was that the drug was used as a sacrament and that this was essential to the exercise of the Indians' religious faith. Eventually, the Native American Church won its case.

A related case involved Dr. Timothy Leary who, when arrested bringing marijuana across the Mexican border into the United States, pleaded that the use of this and other drugs was sacramental in the church he had founded and was essential to the free exercise of his religion. Dr. Leary described drugs as the "sacramental substance" of his new religion. Eventually, the defendant was convicted and the conviction was upheld by higher courts. It was enough for the court that "Congress has demonstrated beyond doubt (by making traffic in marijuana a crime subject to penalties) that it believes marijuana is an evil in American society and a serious threat to its people."

SUNDAY LAWS

An even more significant "free exercise" case involved Sunday laws. This was the case of *Sherbert* v. *Verner* which the Supreme Court decided in 1963. An employer discharged an employee of the Seventh-day Adventist faith because she had refused to work on Saturday, her Sabbath. She applied for unemployment compensation on the ground that she could not obtain employment which did not require her to work on Saturdays. Officials rejected her claim on the ground that her religious scruples did not exempt her from the requirement of accepting available suitable work.

The United States Supreme Court overturned this decision, holding that the denial of unemployment compensation in this case did definitely impede the observance of this religion. The Court found that the ruling forces her to choose between following the precepts of her religion and forfeiting benefits, on the one hand, and abandoning one of the precepts of her religion in order to accept work on the other hand. Governmental imposition of such a choice puts the same kind of burden upon the free exercise of religion as would a fine against appellant for her Saturday worship.

WHAT IS A CHURCH?

Yet another "free exercise" case involved the Ethical Society of Washington, D. C. Although tax exemption was given in the District of Columbia to all houses of worship, the Ethical Society had been denied exemption on the ground that it was not really a church or religious society under the law. But the Court of Appeals ruled that the Society did qualify for tax exemption as a church or religious society. The decisive point was that the Court would not go into the nature of the religious beliefs held by these votaries, even to the point of saying that belief in God was not necessary to qualify as a religious society for tax exemption purposes. The Court explained that to limit tax exemption to orthodox groups would raise constitutional issues under the establishment clause.

THE SUPREME COURT ON RELIGION IN THE SCHOOLS

Two decisions of the United States Supreme Court in the 1960's dealt with the subject of religious observances in the public schools. These were the "Prayer" case, *Engel* v. *Vitale* (1962), and the "Bible Reading" case, *Abington* v. *Schempp* (1963). In *Engel,* the Court considered the New York State Regents' prayer which had been devised by public authorities and made mandatory in New York State schools for all students at the beginning of every school day The prayer was as follows:

> Almighty God, we acknowledge our dependence upon Thee, and we beg Thy blessing upon us, our parents, our teachers and our country.

After the commencement of the litigation a provision was added which stated that any student who did not desire to be present during the prayer might be excused. The Court held that such a mandatory prayer in the public schools was unconstitutional since it trespassed on the Establishment Clause of the First Amendment. Requiring such a prayer as part of a compulsory religious exercise was not permissible even though children could be excused at their own request.

In the *Schempp* case the mandatory reading of a portion of the Bible or the recitation of the Lord's Prayer as part of a religious exercise was forbidden again as an act respecting establishment of religion. It is worth noting that one of the grounds for the decision was the use of public funds for a religious purpose. In his concurring opinion Justice Douglas identified the issue as "whether New York oversteps the bounds when it finances a religious exercise." Justice Douglas then added: "Yet once government finances a religious exercise it inserts a divisive influence into our communities."

There has been a good deal of popular misunderstanding of the Supreme Court decision in the Bible reading and prayer cases. The Court has been accused of "driving God out of the schools," etc. A careful reading of the opinion shows that Bible study itself has not been banned in the schools, nor has the objective study of religion. The singing of anthems which include the composer's profession of faith in God is not affected, nor ceremonial references to God. In a concurring opinion, Justice Brennan indicated that the following activities would be constitutionally permissible: providing chaplains for the military and in penal institutions, exemption of clergy from military service, excusing children from school for religious holidays, and providing temporary use of public buildings for religious sevices when church facilities are unavailable because of an emergency.

THE SUBSIDY ISSUE

One of the crucial issues which the Supreme Court has had to adjudicate has been that of tax support for churches or their institutions. If the Federal Government or a state passed laws providing financial support for church institutions, would this be an act respecting establishment of religion? For many years no such litigation came to the attention of the Court The reason for this was that no laws of this nature had ever been passed. It was the general assumption that church institutions could not be financed from the public treasury. In 1947, this issue, though in a peripheral way, came to the Court. A New Jersey community gave bus fare rebates to students for transportation to school. The rebates were also provided for students in a Roman Catholic school and this practice was challenged as a violation of the First Amendment.

In a 5 to 4 decision the United States Supreme Court upheld the practice. What the Court sought to do was to put school transportation over to the side as a health and safety aid to the child, rather than as a contribution to the school. Had there been under consideration any form of aid to the school itself, the Court said, this would have been struck down as government aid to religion. The key passage from Justice Black's majority opinion reads:

> The "establishment of religion" clause of the First Amendment means at least this: Neither a state nor the Federal Government can set up a church. Neither can pass laws which aid one religion, aid all religions, or prefer one religion over another. Neither can force nor influence a person to go to or remain away from church against his will or force him to profess a belief or disbelief in any religion . . . No tax in any amount, large or small, can be levied to support any religious activities ⸱r institutions, whatever form they may adopt to teach or practice religion.

To underscore its tight "money line" doctrine of church-state separation, the Supreme Court reiterated this very language in *McCollum* v. *Board of Education* and *Torcaso* v. *Watkins.* The language in *Zorach* v. *Clauson* was almost as sweeping. There can scarcely be room for doubt that the Court meant to clamp a tight prohibition on the use of public funds for church schools. Yet *Everson* has provided an opening for churches to try for some public aid for their schools. They could attempt it under the guise of "aid to the child" in the church school rather than aid to the school itself.

THE PROBLEM OF "LACK OF STANDING"

In the 1960's, a series of Federal laws were passed which provided indirect forms of aid to church schools. Separationists sought to challenge these laws in the courts but were frustrated by the problem of "standing to sue." This doctrine enunciated in a 50-year-old case, *Frothingham* v. *Mellon,* held that a taxpayer's interest was not sufficient to challenge constitutionality of Federal expenditures. First Amendment suits were thrown out in dreary succession under the *Frothingham* doctrine.

Finally separationists brought a state case with the idea of appealing it to the United States Supreme Court, thus achieving a hearing on an appeal from a state court which they could not get in a lower Federal Court. The case was *Horace Mann* v. *Maryland Board of*

Public Works. Taxpayers challenged grants of the State of Maryland to four church-related colleges on the ground that they violated the First Amendment. In a 1966 split decision, the Maryland Court of Appeals struck down three of the four grants. It said that three institutions, being organically related to the Methodist and Roman Catholic Churches, could not be subsidized by the State of Maryland. The schools were Western Maryland College, Mount St. Joseph's College and Notre Dame of Maryland. A fourth college, Hood, was judged to have a relationship with the United Church of Christ which was only nominal and not controlling.

The Attorney General of Maryland appealed to the United States Supreme Court but that tribunal refused to hear it. Thus, a church-state showdown was again postponed. To compound the confusion, the three denominational colleges went to the U.S. Office of Education and got Federal grants of the same kind which the Maryland Court had struck down as in violation of the First Amendment! Eventually, this impasse was broken. In *Flast* v. *Cohen,* the United States Supreme Court finally granted standing to taxpayer plaintiffs who desired to challenge Federal expenditures to church institutions. Sectarian aid provisions in Federal aid to education and welfare legislation promptly came under challenge and began to move toward a showdown in the Supreme Court. The 1970's will undoubtedly see the adjudication of many of these cases.

The initial outcome was not reassuring for separationists. *Board of Education* v. *Allen* (1968) represented a challenge to a New York law which authorized use of the State's funds for purchase of textbooks for students in church schools. The law was upheld, Justice White stating that it came in the permissible category of a law having a "secular legislative purpose and a primary legislative effect that neither advances nor inhibits religion." Since the books were not religious in nature and ownership of them remained technically in the public agency, and in view of the fact that plaintiffs failed to show that all teaching in a parochial school was religious, the Court found no church-state violation. What this decision may mean in forecasting the Court's future attitude on church-state questions remains to be seen.

THE WALZ CASE

A welter of cases challenging tax exemption for churches under the establishment clause of the First Amendment is reflected in *Walz* v. *Tax Commission of New York* which reached the United States

Supreme Court late in 1969. Walz, a New York taxpayer, complained that he had to pay more taxes because the churches paid nothing. He said that exempting churches from taxes had exactly the same effect as if the government collected taxes from churches and then rebated them. If this were aid to the churches, then all exemptions should be withdrawn because of the ban on acts respecting establishment of religion. Walz contended that church property should be taxed the same as any other.

The defense countered by showing that tax exemption for churches had a history which ante-dated the First Amendment; also that the state had no obligation to tax all property. The State had always exempted some properties, and taxed others. This was perfectly legal so long as the exemptions were on a nondiscriminatory basis. If religious institutions, with the same kind of standing as other exempt institutions, were to be taxed, this would destroy the "free exercise" of religion. The church exemption had continued in all states for 200 years; to upset it would be profoundly confusing to the nation and disturbing to church-state separation.

THE SUBVERSIVE

CHAPTER VII

THE CHALLENGE TO CHURCH-STATE SEPARATION

There is a clear and serious challenge to the concept of church-state separation today. The challenge is posed by the mounting disposition of government to finance church operations and the willingness of church managers to receive these funds. We see the trend to this kind of state-church interaction most clearly in education, where both Federal and state subsidies have begun to flow to church institutions. But we see it also in health and welfare programs, antipoverty programs, surplus property and commodities disposal, housing and urban redevelopment, and even foreign aid. It has been estimated that as much as $7 billion annually is supplied by government at all levels to churches and their institutions. The voluntary aspect of church support seems to be receding, while support from taxes appears to increase. Pennsylvania, Ohio, Rhode Island and Connecticut have been the first states to provide direct grants for church schools. As constitutional revision becomes the fashion, clerical leaders seek to remove existing provisions which forbid tax support of their church institutions. State legislators are importunated to pass church school subsidy bills.

The fact that establishment of religion is never formalized in any of these arrangements and that carefully fostered fictions obscure it, does not diminish the danger. A "back door establishment" can be quite as complete in time as any other. As Justice Douglas observed: "The best way to establish any institution is to finance it." This creeping rise of religious establishment makes important and necessary a complete re-evaluation of separation of church and state. We must ask whether the principle discovered and enunciated by the Founding Fathers has permanent validity. Is it one of those timeless truths perpetually good through all kinds of shifting changes? Or is it only an accommodation, good for certain times and conditions but no longer viable?

BASIC PREMISES

We assert as our credo that the separation of church and state reaches one of those verities which time and circumstances cannot erode. It is a beacon which keeps flashing insistently at every important intersection in human affairs. Those who ignore its message must suffer the consequences as men have done so often in the past. The truths of church-state separation we assert are relevant to any clime and age.

What are these truths? They include the following:

Religion should be private and voluntary. It should represent the choice of individuals made from free conscience. The coercive power of government should not be used in the realm of religion at all. The state should never compel anyone to go to church or stay away from church, nor to go to a church school. It should never tax any man as much as "three pence" for the support of religion. There should be no tax for religion levied directly or indirectly. All evasions and circumventions by which such aid might be provided should be resolutely rejected. There should be no interlocking of the processes of the churches and the state. They should remain functionally and financially separate.

Government should be strictly neutral in this realm. It should not only refrain from setting up a church or churches, prescribing theologies and the like, it should keep out of this area altogether, making no moves that would either promote or impede religion. Government should do nothing which concerns this, nothing which pertains to this, for religion is an area into which government should not intrude.

Religion should enjoy complete "free exercise." Save for certain general limitations growing out of considerations of health and decency, all persons and groups should have freedom to meet, evangelize, collect funds, acquire property, erect houses of worship and hold title to them, promote and advance their beliefs among the populace. Every citizen should have complete freedom to make his own decision in regard to religion or to ignore religion, quite free of coercion.

Government should never penalize anyone because of his religious beliefs or lack of them. The clergy should enjoy full political rights in common with all citizens, but they should not use their holy office to coerce the political process. No citizen should be handicapped or given an advantage before the law because of his religious faith.

While no concept of human or institutional relations can be said to be "absolute" in the total sense of the word, the concept of separation of church and state approaches this as nearly as any other. This is

42

true because the freedom which we cherish appears to require separation of church and state as an essential ingredient. The assumption that religion lies outside the purview of government automatically makes separation a principle of the most pervasive nature.

Church-state separation is essential for the health of religion. The saddest chapters in the history of religion have been recorded when a union of church and state estranged the church from the people and robbed it of its strength and vitality.

Our Founders felt that only when necessary to prevent some immediate peril to the state should any infringement on religious freedom be permitted and then only to the extent necessary to avert that peril.

There can be no doubt that separation of church and state in America is a plan not only sound in principle but sound in practice. It has been good for both the church and the state. Let us keep it so.

FREE ENTERPRISE– AN AMERICAN INVENTION

by

HAROLD M. FLEMING

Edited by

ROBERT B. WATTS, 33°, G∴C∴
Director of Education

1

GEORGE WASHINGTON

BY

HORATIO GREENOUGH, 1840

"The sculptor intended this massive work to honor America's 'great example of liberty' and symbolize attainment of a freedom in which the arts, sciences, and technology would flourish."

Smithsonian Institution

3

TABLE OF CONTENTS

FOREWORD

The ancient Grecian Credo was "know thyself." I suppose the American Creed is "do thy stuff." We adore doers. We are a Nation of doers. We applaud those men in public life and in Science who typify energetic action. In the field of public affairs: Franklin, Washington, Andrew Jackson, Theodore Roosevelt. In the field of Science: Fulton of the steamboat, Morse of the telegraph, Bell of the telephone, Burbank, the Wright brothers, and the great bridge builder Joseph B. Strauss.

From babyhood we dream of improvement and invention. We were peopled by enterprising immigrants. They became imbued with ideals of self-support and self-help, unknown to the class-conscious old world.

America made the machine age. A typical textbook, William M. West's "The Story Of Our Country," remarks that "The American invents as the Greek chiseled, as the Venetian painted, as the Italian sang." Lincoln told the apocryphal story of the Massachusetts baby, six months old, sitting upon its mother's lap, viewing its own cradle, to see if it could not invent a better one!

We are indeed happy, therefore, to present this fourth volume in our New Series of Dynamic Freedoms. It tells in a straightforward manner the exciting story of the American invention of individual freedom and enterprise as a basic concept of government. It describes in simple and understandable language the tremendous achievements which follow from that freedom, and points out the almost limitless opportunities which lie before our young people of today.

Before making changes in that typically American system, we should understand how our free enterprise system works. Often the proposed changes are based on a lack of knowledge of the vital methods that are necessary for a continuance of success.

This booklet is thus a much-needed guide and is really a challenge to us for even greater achievements in the future.

Sovereign Grand Commander

5

CHAPTER 1

FREEDOM

THE MATERIAL ACHIEVEMENT

Everybody knows the tremendous material advance this country has made since World War II. Nearly everybody knows it by having shared in it. The current of energy that flows through American work and play has increased fast in the last 25 years.

But these postwar economic gains are only the latest installment of an American achievement that has been under way for more than 180 years. Since the signing of the United States Constitution, the American economic system has been growing at the same rate as in the last quarter-century.

And as these economic gains have been adding to each other, decade after decade, like compound interest, the result has been more material progress in 180 years than in the previous 1,800 years.

When this all began, everyday life in American towns and cities was not much different from everyday life in the towns and cities of the Roman empire. The similarity was even greater on the farm, where most people lived. Tools and methods had changed little in 2,000 years. Then, rapidly, they began to change.

THE POLITICAL ACHIEVEMENT

With this material progress, we have also had our political freedom—the greatest of non-material, spiritual values. In this country's history, more people have been free to mind their own business, and have had fewer people to mind their business for them, than in almost any other place or time in human history. Millions of Europeans came here, not in search of material wealth, for this country at first had little of it, but because this was a "land of liberty" and of opportunity.

We Americans are inclined to take for granted this combination of material progress and of personal liberty. But the assumption that they go together is being challenged today all over the world—and

6

FREEDOM

even in this country. The contrary idea is spreading, helped by the Russians, that economic progress and political freedom *cannot go together*. A new fashion of thinking says that nations must make a choice between the one or the other—progress *or* freedom. The idea is that the two are incompatible—that a nation cannot have both at the same time.

In fact some people carry the idea even further. They say that it is *only* material economic progress that can lead to freedom. The Russians, for instance, say that they will outgrow us in *economics,* meaning that *after that* (perhaps) they will have *political freedom.* And some of the under-developed countries say that they are too poor to enjoy freedom of enterprise (or in some cases even freedom of speech.)

This is diametrically opposite to American experience and history.

The United States started as an under-developed country. It had no net capital. It was heavily in debt and operating on borrowed money. It had no railroads, no factories, no steel mills, nor any other kind of sizeable "capital accumulation."

In fact it had only one real asset of any importance. And this was not an economic asset at all, but a political one. Many other countries were far ahead of us in the major economic assets of the day—ships, roads, machinery, skilled labor, coal, iron, gold and silver. This country's almost unique asset was the idea of a meticulously limited government. It was written into the Constitution. It was put most briefly in the Bill of Rights. It was the reverse of the European idea that a "Government knows best." It was the idea of freedom not only from George the Third's government, but from *any government.*

THE INVENTION OF FREEDOM

The idea of individual freedom, *as a general good in itself,* on which this country was founded, and from which the American achievement started, was an *invention.* It was as new in its day as the telephone, the gasoline engine, or the first frozen foods were in their day.

It was the product of many men's thoughts and struggles. Its invention was a long story, and, for us a lucky historic accident. The final breakthrough came only after centuries of trial-and-error. We have the English largely to thank for it.

7

FREEDOM

Historians trace the river of our forefathers' ideas about freedom back at least 750 years, to the English Magna Carta of 1215 A.D. This was a written statement of rights against the Crown, which the feudal barons exacted from King John at Runnymede, up the Thames River from London. Its most famous clause was that:—

"No freeman shall be imprisoned or dispossessed. . . unless by the lawful judgment of his equals, or by the law of the land."

These words had the same meaning then as if, in the twentieth century they had been forced upon Germany's Hitler, Russia's Kremlin chiefs, Cuba's Castro, or Mao Tse-Tung and his henchmen.

And the rights thus written down came to be known as "the immemorial rights of Englishmen."

The feudal barons were later replaced by national governments in Spain, France, and England. And these governments, as is the nature of governments, took to economic planning. Under the "mercantilist" idea, they tried to regulate everything they could control—exports, imports, wages, production, prices, etc. They granted monopolies and supported privileges.

To our everlasting fortune in this country, the English government was the least efficient and least determined of these governments. Queen Elizabeth, the Cal Coolidge of her day, answered most economic problems by doing nothing about them. Charles I's pretensions got him

WE MUST BE FREE TO INVENT.

beheaded. Cromwell's absolutism ended the Commonwealth. James II's programs got him exiled. Magna Carta was revived.

Meantime, colonizing the New World became the growth industry of its time. And, true to form, the Spanish and French governments tried to run their colonies as government ventures, but the less ambitious English government gave its colonists little more than a charter and its blessing. The English colonies were private ventures, free to sink or swim on their own.

And on their own, they soon began to swim mightily. They had put 3,000 miles of the Atlantic Ocean between them and the European hodge-podge of feudal-inherited, or government-protected, privileges, monopolies, customs and restrictions.

In the New World, the farmer no longer had to live in town and decide next year's planting program in committee. He could move out, live in the middle of his farm, and run it as he pleased, raising such crops as he chose, either for himself or for the market. The English-born workman in the New World was free to move about, to charge what wages he could get, or to set up his own shop. And the colonial merchant was free to buy and sell wherever, whenever, and at whatever prices he saw fit. These were new and heady freedoms.

After the colonists began to thrive, the British government began trying to fit them into its economic plans. They didn't fit very well. George III came to the throne in 1760. He was conscientious and German in his planning for his subjects. Among other things he decided that the American colonists should not move over the Appalachians. Eventually the colonists revolted, not as Americans but as Englishmen. And up came Magna Carta again. For instance, the Massachusetts Assembly in declaring the Stamp Act void, said that it was "against Magna Carta and the natural rights of Englishmen, and therefore . . . void."

Thus the "immemorial rights of Englishmen," transplanted to the edge of the wilderness, became the "natural rights of Americans, *against the Crown.*"

These rights were sometimes separately defined, as freedom of conscience, freedom of speech, freedom of movement and freedom of property. But their histories all ran parallel. And by the time of the Revolution, they were recognized as interrelated and as essentially all the same thing—freedom from government interference. Thus free men recognized what all totalitarian governments recognize, that the rights of conscience, association, speech and property, rise and fall together. A government that can shut a man's mouth can also take his property, and vice versa.

Until this time, in all Western history, the basic political idea had been that the government should have all rights except those specifically granted to citizens. But now, for the first time, this idea was inverted. Citizens should have all rights except those specifically granted to the government.

This was such an historic breakthrough that Tom Paine, the voice of the American Revolution, wrote in his "Common Sense" pamphlet:—

"We have it in our power to begin the world over again. A situation, similar to the present, hath not happened since the days of Noah until now."

(In fact you can see this bold idea still being engraved on the back of every dollar bill. The great Seal of the United States says "NOVUS ORDO SECLORUM"—"A New Order of the Ages.")

And the Founding Fathers wrote this unprecedented, upside-down idea of government into the United States Constitution. They framed the weakest government they thought could fill the barest essential needs for a government.

THE "BUSINESS END" OF THE CONSTITUTION

Into this Constitution the authors put an assurance that a man could own his own inventions and writings for a limited time (Article 1, Section 8); that the States should not issue paper money (Article 1, Section 10); that the States should not pass any law abridging the obligation of contract (Article 1, Section 10); that this Nation would be a common market (Article 1, Section 10); and that (echoing Magna Carta) no person should be deprived of his property without due process of law (Article 5, Bill of Rights).

These are the so-called "business clauses" of the Constitution. They opened the way for the free enterprise which has produced the American economic achievement. They led to economic adventure, competition, obsolescence, and sharing.

Let us consider these results in the chapters that follow.

CHAPTER 2

ADVENTURE

ONE GROWTH INDUSTRY AFTER ANOTHER

The ink was hardly dry on the United States Constitution in 1787, when the country began to see such a rapid flowering of the industrial arts as had never been seen before in human history.

The new political ideas of the Founding Fathers promptly began to pay off like the research ideas of a growth industry. It was as though a switch had been thrown, and a current of new energy introduced into the American circuit.

For generation after generation of Americans, the progress that followed was much like the progress we have seen in the last two decades. Each generation was as astonished as the present one by the changes it saw. There was as much excitement 150 years ago about steamboats as there is today about travel in outer space; and as much turmoil 100 years ago about new methods of packaging food as there is today.

The new nation began to develop a series of growth industries. They were based on new inventions. The first such growth industry was cotton-raising. Eli Whitney invented the cotton gin in 1793; within a decade cotton production had multiplied ten times. Then, as growth industries, there came in succession steamboating, railroading, farming, textile manufacturing, and steel production. Each, for a time, grew tremendously.

INVENTORS IN ODD CORNERS

These industries started from inventions and combinations of inventions. The inventions generally grew out of the ideas of eccentric thinkers, working long hours in obscure places on odd ideas. Most of these men were of what eighteenth-century Englishmen would have called "lower-class origin." Thus:—

Alexander Graham Bell was a speech teacher to a deaf mute pupil, and his first financing was from her father, a shoe manufacturer.

11

ADVENTURE

Thomas Edison started as a railroad newsboy, and was once thrown off a train for setting it on fire with a chemical experiment.

Henry Ford failed in business twice before the Ford Motor Company began to succeed.

Orville and Wilbur Wright ran a bicycle shop.

And the first American to seal processed tomatoes in tin cans was a gardener, H. W. Crosby.

Yet many of these men's names are great in American history. In the history of most nations, the famous names are those of kings, ministers, generals, and noblemen. The United States Constitution says that "No title of nobility shall be granted by the United States." But here are some of the noble names in American history: Whitney; duPont; Fulton; McCormick; Case; Deere; Morse; Lowell; Colt; Pullman; Gatling; Borden; Westinghouse; Bell; Remington; Underwood; Eastman; Edison; Ford; and Wright. Inventors all.

And here are some of the more important inventions during the middle of the nineteenth century:

In the 1830's—the mowing machine, the reaper, the harvester, the revolver, the magnetic telegraph, and vulcanized rubber.

In the 1840's—the turret lathe, the sewing machine, the rotary printing press, and the safety pin.

In the 1850's—the ice-making machine, evaporated milk, the Mason jar, and the Pullman car.

In the 1860's—the machine gun, the typewriter, and the railroad air-brake.

In the 1870's—celluloid, the gasoline engine, barbed wire, the telephone, the phonograph, the disc cultivator, the incandescent lamp, and the cash register.

In the 1880's—the trolley car, the fountain pen, the Linotype, the electrolytic process for making aluminum, the safety bicycle, and the Kodak.

THE FINANCING OF INVENTIONS

The marvel of the new economics was not (and is not, today) that so many things got invented, but that so many inventions reached the public. Free men are naturally inventive; but there never before

12

was such a follow-through. Previous history is full of lost inventions. The ancient Greeks measured the circumference of the earth and invented a steam engine over 2,000 years ago. In renaissance Italy, Leonardo da Vinci is credited with 21 inventions. But until modern times most inventions were soon forgotten unless, like gunpowder, they were put to military use. There was nobody to risk the money on financing them.

One reason for the outburst of inventions was the patent system— itself an invention. It gave the inventor, in exchange for publicly explaining his idea, 17 years of full property rights in it.

More important—nobody could legally stop the inventor, or his backers, from putting his idea on the market. He need not go before an official board, which might turn thumbs down on his idea, either because it "wouldn't work," or because the board feared it might work all too well and so put somebody out of business or out of a job. Through previous history, this had been a major hazard to inventors, that they might be stopped because their ideas might endanger existing jobs or investments.

PROGRESS INEVITABLY OUTMODES "THE LATEST THING."

But the main reason for the flood of newly invented products was that, with this temporary property right in ideas, a profit might be hoped for from pushing them. If the inventor had no money—and he generally hadn't—others could put up the money and share in the hopes. The unique new force was not invention, but private venture money or "risk-capital."

ADVENTURE

In former centuries, well-to-do people had never had such opportunities to risk their money in new ideas, except, in some cities, in shipping ventures. Profits had been frowned on. Contracts had had little legal support. Government might obstruct such ventures, or take the winnings. And it was considered beneath a 'gentleman" to go into "trade." So wealth had gone into "conspicuous consumption"—lace cuffs, servants, castles and fountains.

But, as freedom was the major economic breakthrough of the eighteenth century, so the financing of new ideas was one of the chief developments of the nineteenth century.

When James Watt, in 1769, was working on an improved reciprocating steam engine, he had plenty of ideas, but no money. But a Matthew Boulton, going into partnership with Watt, put up, eventually, the $150,000 needed. And ever since then, the cost of getting inventions to market has been met by various kinds of cooperation between inventors and monied persons. During the nineteenth century, all kinds of new financial devices were worked out to enlist adventure-capital in new ideas. One of the earlier sources of money was the "merchant banker." A later source was the "joint-stock company," which raised money by selling its shares and bonds to a growing investor public.

Among others, a new man appeared on the scene—the promoter, or "entrepreneur," as later economists called him. He made a business of bringing together inventions, capital, and customers.

The late Wendell Willkie once explained how this worked out in one typical growth industry—electric power. He said:

'In the beginning there was the development by Edison of the incandescent lamp. No official set him at it and none passed on it.

"Then he issued licenses to use it. They were taken up by men in private enterprise. Ambitious fellows, who couldn't sleep of nights, took it out to the towns and tried to raise money to install it. For 25 years they hoped, risked, made and lost. The early story of the utility business is that it was started, nursed, got going, and then made to grow, by men willing to risk their own money, who took their enterprises to bed with them and stayed awake nights thinking up where to find money to feed the business, equipment to produce and transmit the power, and customers to replenish the till."

In all these ventures, the hope of profit was the driving force. It may not have inspired the inventor, but it inspired the people who put

14

up the money. The result has been called "the profit system." But it is better called the *"hope-of-profit* system," or the *"profit-and-loss* system." For the road was strewn with failures. Only a fraction of the new ideas paid off.

MASS PRODUCTION FOR THE MASSES

Among the new devices were powerdrives (first water-power and then steam power) and interchangeable parts. And so, as machines got better, *mass production* followed.

Mass production began with guns and clocks. The first *big* mass production was in textiles, where cheap water-power was available along the "fall line" of the Atlantic Coast rivers.

Mass production required two things. One was mass markets, which naturally meant, with the "masses." The other was large amounts of risk capital.

The rise of mass production, however, also depended on the development of what is now one of the basic economic principles of American business. This is the principle of larger *total* profits, from smaller *unit* profits. It is sometimes called the "reach for volume." It might be explained as follows:

A company has a new product, and the managers are figuring how to make the most money out of it. They think:

(1) "With a small plant, our engineers think we could make 1,000,000 pounds of this product a year for 50¢ a pound. And our market research people estimate we could sell this 1,000,000 pounds for $1.00 a pound. Result: annual profit of 50¢ a pound on 1,000,000 pounds, equals $500,000.

(2) "But our market research people think that if we could *get the price down to 40¢ we could sell 10,000,000* pounds. And our engineers estimate that with a plant big enough to make that much a year, they could get the cost down to 20¢ a pound. Result: annual profit of 20¢ a pound on 10,000,000 pounds, or $2,000,000, or four times the profit at 40¢ as at $1.00."

This is much over-simplified, but it expresses the principle that has been followed in great areas of American business. The most famous example was that of Henry Ford, who cut the price of a new car from $950 to $500, and eventually to $290, raised wages, and still made great profits. The same principle has been followed in such leading American businesses as electric power, gasoline, food distribution, chemicals and canmaking.

But success in this reach for volume is not simple. It involves large risks with large amounts of money. Many firms have gone bankrupt this way. Nineteenth century Socialists used to think that the new factory owner merely figured his costs, added a markup for profit, and then roped in the money. But the joker in that view is shown above, in such phrases as "our engineers *think* . . ." and "our market people *estimate* . . ." Every plant is built on nothing more than "educated guesses."

Nor does the above show all the pitfalls in capital investment for mass production. Another is that if the company builds too large, the excess or unused capacity will eat up the profits, in interest costs, depreciation, maintenance and other unproductive "overhead costs." A big plant, like a horse in a stable, eats whether it works or not.

Still another important calculation must be made before one builds a plant. How long will the market last for its product? Will the customers want something else before your plant investment can pay for itself? For instance glass, metal and plastics have on occasion replaced each other as containers for certain products. In airline operations propeller planes have been replaced by jets, and these in turn in some cases by the giant new "air buses." Computers are already in their third "generation"—the first generation of computers having been built around tubes, the second one with simple transistors, and the third generation with more "sophisticated" semi-conductors. And with each such "generation gap" much expensive manufacturing equipment is outmoded.

HOW TO KEEP MAKING MONEY

The ideal way for a company to keep up in a free economy is for it to keep finding new products to make that people want, or new uses for existing products; and then to figure, somewhere nearly correctly, how many of the new products or applications it can sell, at what cost, and for how long (before they are outmoded).

This is one main reason for the enormous growth in recent years of research and development.

It is a fantasy of European origin that profits are normally made by hiring people cheap and selling their products dear. In a limited

16

way, and in certain circumstances, this can be done. There will always be sweatshops. And it is true that many successful nineteenth century employers and promoters were about as "social-minded" as a Maine-coast lobster. But the one who made "real money" did not do it by "squeezing the faces of the poor." They did it by bringing to market new ideas, new machines, new products, or new services. They were adventurers and innovators. And the clue to their money-making was good judgment in anticipating what the customer might want, in what amounts, at what prices, and for how long. From this, combined with their cost-cutting, they got a profit.

CHAPTER 3

COMPETITION

FREE MARKETS

The business of America depends on free and open markets. The nation's economic life could not go on without them, except with tremendous waste and delay.

There are hundreds of these markets, big and little. Some of the best known and largest ones, like the New York Stock Exchange and the Chicago Board of Trade, handle a huge volume of bids and offers that come in constantly by telephone and telegraph. They operate like continuous auctions, and in fact many such large markets are called "auction markets."

But there are hundreds of smaller and slower markets. Some are called "over-the-counter markets." Some are merely "telephone markets." Some are "quoted markets." There are local markets as well as national markets. There are specialied markets for scores of such commodities as 92-octane gasoline, cadmium, platinum and polyethylene. Open most trade magazines, and you will find they carry a special page on "The Current Markets."

Only three things are required to make a market. One is that buyers and sellers have contact. They needn't be present in person in a market place; but they must have some means of knowing the course of prices, even if it only by telegraph or in a trade paper. A second is that the market is open to any would-be buyer or seller. The third, and most important, is that prices are free to move up and down without restraint. If prices are controlled, "the market" is destroyed; and buyers and sellers then turn to a "black market."

Market prices constantly adjust supply to demand. If there is too much supply, buyers back away until the price drops. If it drops too low, buyers come in again, but suppliers drop out. This keeps the goods moving from where they can be most cheaply produced, to where they are most wanted. Free prices work as a valve, or governor, on production and consumption.

COMPETITION

In contrast, when prices are controlled, supply and demand promptly get out of adjustment. We have had plenty of examples of this in recent years. During World War II, the price of such things as sugar was held down by government control. The result was to discourage and slow down supply, but to increase demand. This led to a shortage, which led to rationing.

On the other hand many farm prices have been held *up* in recent years by government action. The result has been to stimulate production, but to discourage consumption. This has led to billions of dollars' worth of surpluses, which eat up storage charges and finally have to be given away or "dumped" abroad, at prices even lower than they might have brought in a free market.

FREE COMPETITION

Free markets imply free competition. The two are really one and the same thing. Competition must be unobstructed by attempts at monopoly, conspiracy, or restraint of trade, with or without government blessing.

The Sherman Antitrust Act of 1890 prohibited conspiracies from restraining trade, and monopolizing—or 'attempting to monopolize."

Many people assume that it is vigilant enforcement of this Act that makes American business competitive. But this is so only in the same way that policemen keep us honest.

Free competition is one of the heritages of the American economy. It was one of the goals of the Founding Fathers. Monopolies and trade restraints, imposed on the colonists, were one of the principal causes of the Revolution.

And Americans have always had more faith in open "hard" competition than Europeans. This is still so today.

HORSE-AND-BUGGY COMPETITION

Competition has been increasing in this country throughout its history. It has increased particularly with every advance in communication and transportation. Each of these has widened the markets to include more and more sellers as well as more and more buyers.

At first, competition was slow. Markets were local. In frontier communities, monopoly of a sort was inevitable. There was only one cobbler, one blacksmith and one "General Store," just as in some towns

19

COMPETITION

today there is only one movie and one weekly newspaper. Goods didn't move far. Perhaps the first important competition was that of the early travelling peddlers, cobblers and tinsmiths.

It was turnpikes, canals, steamboats and railroads that first widened markets and spread competition. The new manufacturing companies began to send around "drummers" who travelled by rail from city to city and "beat the drum" for their employers' goods. Then came the mail-order houses and the department stores.

AMERICAN BUSINESS TRIES MONOPOLY

From 1860 to 1900, mills and factories were springing up all over the northeastern United States. The leading growth industry was steel, using the new Bessemer process. But scores of other industries were growing rapidly out of the handicraft stage, through invention and machinery, into a heavily competitive stage.

As the competition in these industries got tougher and rougher, it often threatened to wipe out profits altogether. Even railroads sometimes cut tariffs competitively to the point of bankruptcy. Members of many industries tried to put a stop to this strenuous price competition. They used various devices. The most popular was to set up a "trust," controlled by a small board of directors, into which competitors would put the controlling stocks of their own companies.

To cope with this, Congress passed the Sherman Act in 1890. But there was little machinery for enforcement, and in 1897 the Supreme Court made the now strange-sounding decision that a monopoly in *production* was not necessarily a monopoly in *sale and distribution*. This seemed to give a green light to another anti-competitive device— the putting together of competitors into a single company. By 1901 scores of such combinations were put together, with names beginning with such words as Allied, Amalgamated, American, Consolidated, International, National, United, and United States—the biggest of them all being the United States Steel Corporation, a giant in its time with a capitalization of $1,400,000,000. These companies combined from 60 to over 90 per cent of the manufacturing capacity in their respective industries.

When the historic smoke had cleared, it showed few successes among the expensive attempts at monopoly. Within 20 years it was obvious that competition could not be so abruptly choked down. Some of these companies kept on trying to restrain trade, and were broken

20

up by the courts. Of the others, many failed financially. The rest survived to rank among the nation's most successful corporations. But they did so only by efficiency and first-class management, and by trying to keep ahead of the competition, not to restrain it. The supposed benefits of monopoly proved a mirage. Even the successful survivors rapidly lost ground to competitors, and ended up with 25 to 40 per cent of the business, instead of 70 to 90 per cent.

COMPETITION IN NEW DIMENSIONS

Twentieth-century competition in American industry has intensified far beyond anything known in the nineteenth century. There have been several causes for this.

1. Competition Between Industries. At the turn of the century, competition was still largely inside particular industries. Cotton mills competed with cotton mills, steel mills with steel mills and can manufacturers among themselves.

But in this century, the progress of the industrial arts has swept like a rising tide over these industry compartments. Cotton competes with synthetic fibers. Oil and natural gas compete with coal. Steel competes with aluminum, copper, plastics and cement. You can have your house built of wood, metal, composition, plastics or pre-stressed concrete. No manufacturer knows where the competition may come from next.

Even legal monopolies have lost ground to this *inter*-industry competition. The telegraph has lost to the telephone and the air mail, the streetcar to the bus and the private car; and the railroad to highway trucks and airlines.

2. Research and Development. The inventions of the nineteenth century came out of woodsheds and workshops. In 1928 American industry spent only $100 million on research and development. By 1945 it was spending nine times as much, and by the 1960's, several billions a year. "R & D" is a "fighting competitive weapon" that may be used both defensively and offensively. As defense, it protects a company from technological surprise. As offense, it may lead a company into entirely new territory. For it follows no conventional industry lines.

Also, manufacturing methods have improved to where it is sometimes said that "anybody can make anything." During World War II automobile manufacturers made tanks, planes, and gyroscopes. Today they could doubtless make textiles, missiles or motors. There are no longer any sheltered industries. It is no longer of important advantage to be a big fish in a small pond.

3. *"Discretionary Income."* Around 1900, most families had to scrape to house, clothe and feed themselves. They had little discretion in their budgets, and most manufacturing competition was in supplying these families with the necessities of life. But today's working families can afford a wide range of purchases beyond the bare necessities. So manufacturers of such varied things as garbage disposal units, hi-fi and stereo, camping equipment, outboard motors and do-it-yourself kits, are all in competition for these "discretionary dollars." They also compete with the savings bank.

4. *"Non-Price" Competition.* As the American standard of living has risen, American business has turned more and more to providing something over and above standard goods at the lowest possible prices. To straight price-competition it has added competition in quality, service, reliability, diversity of product, packaging and so on. This adds dimension to competition.

GOVERNMENT RESTRAINTS OF TRADE

The American free economy started as a revolt against monopolies and other restraints on competition. And through the decades the competition has naturally become more keen.

But history shows that monopolies and restraints of trade have a strong appeal. They are the framework of most economic systems outside ours. They are turned to, particularly, when the competition gets severe.

This story has told how American business tried to restrain its own competition around the turn of the century—and how the attempt wasn't successful. In the 1930's Americans again turned toward restraints on competition. This time it was with government support. Its effects were more permanent.

In the beginning, it was partly the doing of business itself. As the Great Depression deepened in 1931, business groups appealed to President Hoover for some officially-protected system of holding prices. He refused. But in 1933 this idea became the germ of the National Recovery Act. "NRA" exempted business groups from the Sherman Antitrust Act if they would sign "code agreements" with the government on minimum prices and wages.

COMPETITION

"NRA" was thrown out by the Supreme Court in 1935, and by that time was breaking down anyway, as individualist businessmen refused to toe the price lines. But the spirit of controls was in the air. During the long hard times of the 1930's, Congress extended the force of government to many programs to protect various groups in the country from the pressures of free competition.

These programs worked precisely contrary to the spirit of the Sherman Antitrust Act. What the antitrust laws made it illegal to *do,* these laws made it illegal *not to do.*

Today two major results are clear. One is that one such restraint of trade leads politically to another. When one group has protection, another wants it. And so, just as *without* government protection, restraints of trade eventually defeat themselves, so *with* government protection, they multiply.

The other obvious result is that such government-enforced programs to hold up prices, continually raise as many problems as they seem to solve. The government spends billions, with one hand to buy up useless production, and with the other to pay producers not to produce.

In brief, a nation that turns to using its government to protect certain groups from the hardships of competition, is like an alcoholic, for whom "one drink is too much, and a thousand drinks are not enough." The process is a one-way street. Such protection creates vested interests against the rest of the community. If everybody were protected, adventure and competition would end. So would progress.

CHAPTER 4

OBSOLESCENCE

PART 1 — JOB DISPLACEMENT

LEAST TALKED ABOUT

Of all subjects in economics, obsolescence is the least talked about. People talk about the weather but don't do anything about it. They have to do something about obsolescence, but they don't talk much about it. For it is an unhappy subject. It means throwing away good household equipment, doing without the skills of good workmen and scrapping machinery that still has years of useful life. The trouble with all these things is not that they are of no value, but that they are of *comparatively* no value. Progress has outmoded them.

So it isn't strange that about the only people who really like to talk about obsolescence, at least in print, are the machine-tool builders, who have been advertising for a generation that "You pay for better tools, whether you buy them or not. For if your competitors buy them, it will cost you more than if you bought them yourself."

"Obsolete" is a twentieth-century word. Even economists weren't using it in 1899. The nearest common term is the womenfolk's phrase, "out-of-fashion," but this is not quite it. A better synonym is "out-moded." Anyway, obsolescence has had more meaning in this country than anywhere else, and in this century more than ever before. Here is an example.

Let us say that a man bought a new car for $2,000 just after World War II. He never drove it. He put it on jacks, and spent the necessary money each year to keep it in mint condition. Yet after 25 years, how much is it worth? Somewhere perhaps between $100 and $500; dealers' books don't go back that far. The car is hopelessly outmoded. (Meantime, his $2,000 at 4 per cent would have compounded to $5,320.)

24

OBSOLESCENCE

But while the value was drained almost entirely out of this modern vehicle in 25 years, consider, in contrast, what was perhaps the most famous of all nineteenth-century vehicles, celebrated by Oliver Wendell Holmes in his poem about "The Deacon's Masterpiece":

> *"Have you heard of the wonderful one-hoss shay*
> *That was built in such a logical way*
> *It ran a hundred years to a day?"*
> —Oliver Wendell Holmes (1809-1894)

Or take a more familiar example. Our car-buyer's wife in 1947 bought a $350 television set. Today it wouldn't be worth replacing a picture tube. It has been pushed clear out of date.

Obsolescence is the other side of economic progress. The faster a nation's progress, the faster its obsolescence. If you stand in the front of a train, with the engineer, you see progress. If you stand at the rear of the train, you see what's being left behind.

The train moves faster today than ever before. But even in the nineteenth century, when it had got under way, economists hadn't realized the importance of obsolescence. In a Dictionary of Political Economy, published in 1899, consisting of three volumes of about 700 pages each, the word "obsolescence" is not in the index.

Obsolescence appears in three forms—consumer-goods obsolescence; job obsolescence; and machine- or plant-obsolescence.

Consumer obsolescence is the car, television set, ice box, rug-beater, and crystal set that nobody wants. It is "the stuff in the attic" that some people find so hard to throw away. It is the "perfectly good" refrigerators that go to the dump.

Job obsolescence is what has been happening for 150 years, at increasing speed, to such trades as spinning, weaving, flat-boating, teamstering, blacksmithing, and harness-making.

Plant obsolescence is what has happened to most of the factories, mills, railroad lines, airplanes, and machine tools built in this country before World War II. They have been all but completely outmoded and replaced as American business has since that time invested *two-thirds of a trillion dollars* in new plant and equipment.

JOB DISPLACEMENT

There is no job displacement in a static society; but it is always going on in a progressive society. Neither technological unemployment

25

nor automation are new. Automation is only a new word for the mechanization that has been going on for a century.

Consider, for instance, some of the names of people you know—(Smith, Taylor, Shoemaker, Potter or Wright). These are trades. But most of these trades are gone. There are no more blacksmiths, wainwrights (wagon-builders), or wheelwrights.

Or consider what has happened to farming. Once eight out of ten Americans lived on farms. Now it is *one* out of ten. Deep forests now cover a multitude of "cellar holes" in back-country New England—the melancholy sole remaining evidence of once bustling farmhouses of a century ago whose owners finally quit when the railroads opened up the west to grain fields far more fertile than New England hillsides.

There are many possible causes for job obsolescence. Sometimes they are labor-saving devices, as, recently, in coal-mining, steel-making, railroading, and automobile manufacture. But sometimes customers turn away from whole industries. Grandpa used to go to vaudeville, even when there were silent movies. But sound movies ended the jobs of thousands of vaudeville troupers—and of theatre musicians. Some of the actors and musicians then found work in radio. Then television dealt a heavy blow to both movie and radio jobs.

"STOP THE MACHINES!"

From the earliest days of the free economy, new machines have periodically wrought havoc with jobs, sometimes in whole areas. For instance, a century ago they hit particularly hard in England, which was not growing as this country is and where workmen did not have the "mobility" or get-up-and-go that Americans have. The early English textile machinery ended the jobs of whole counties of spinners and weavers. The plight of these depressed areas was far worse than anything we know today in this country, for the displaced craftsmen lived close to starvation anyway, and there was practically no available relief. So they rioted, and broke up many of the new machines. So the government put down the riots and protected the machines.

But this was not the first time that machines were destroyed for their efficiency. A hundred years before Fulton's steamboat sailed the Hudson, a steamboat on the upper Rhine in Germany was destroyed by Rhine river boatmen. And in fact from the days of Rome, inventions had failed of acceptance as much because they would destroy jobs as because they lacked development capital.

OBSOLESCENCE

It is only in the last two centuries, and only in this country, in Great Britain, and in countries that have followed these two nations' principles, that the government and public opinion have sided with the right of inventors and investors to put their products on the market even though this caused consumers to switch away from higher-cost handicraft products.

NEW JOBS—WHERE AND WHEN?

Technological progress can only outmode jobs by first creating new ones. It can only make jobs, machines, or whole industries obsolescent by first creating new jobs, machines or industries.

Today new jobs may not at first be as many as the old ones. But eventually progress creates more jobs than it replaces.

The new jobs normally develop in "growth industries," which are developing new inventions and discoveries into mass production, and so are bidding for help.

However, new industries don't keep "growing to the sky." And there may come a stage where an industry, by continued mechanization, automation, etc., provides steadily fewer jobs. This has happened in the last quarter century, for instance, in steel-making, automobile manufacture, and railroading.

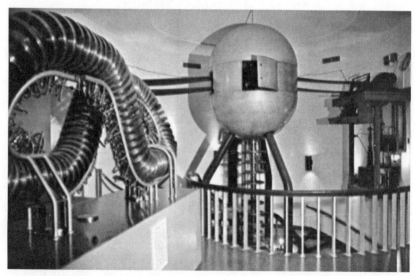

EARLY ATOM SMASHER IN THE SMITHSONIAN

27

On the other hand there are hundreds of thousands more jobs today in such growth industries as electronics, television, books and education, aircraft manufacture, plastics, and the service industries in general, than a quarter century ago.

To hear some people talk, one would think that technological unemployment was a cumulative thing. This is like looking out the rear of the train instead of the front; if it were so there would hardly be anybody working today. But an economic system that is constantly outmoding jobs does so only by constantly creating new ones. Each generation has its own growth industries.

In the last analysis it is the customer who is responsible for technological unemployment. It is he, or she, who has switched buying from one product to another, or to products made cheaper by new machinery and methods.

However, the employer is usually in the same boat with the workman whom he lets go. Wherever a job is outmoded today, it is fairly safe to assume that some rather expensive plant or machinery has also been outmoded. And if the employer doesn't do something about it, he too will eventually be out of a job—that is, out of business.

PART 2 — VANISHING VALUES

INVESTOR BEWARE!

All the plant and equipment built in the nineteenth century, and a good part of what was built in the twentieth century has lost all value, and for the most part has been demolished.

This is not because it wore out, but because it went out of date. It could no longer be used effectively in competing for the customer's dollars.

In one way, property rights are carefully protected in the United States. The Constitution prescribes in Articles 5 and 14 that no one may be deprived of his property except by "due process of law." That means that neither federal nor state governments may take a man's property except for a legal purpose and at a fair price.

But property values in this country have normally no defense against *competition*. Nowhere so fast as in the United States can the value of a man's property be invisibly drained away from him by the progress of the industrial arts.

These two rules are diametrically opposite to the rules of most economic systems in the past. In most countries, for most of human history, property values have been vulnerable to government but protected against competition. In this country they have been protected against government but vulnerable to competition.

Yet this is as it should be, if we are to have economic progress. It is a basic rule of a process, sometimes called "creative destruction," which brings us steady economic gains, but in doing so, steadily wipes out invested values.

The immediate causes of plant and machine obsolescence are varied. Their product may be out of date; a third of what people spend today is for products unknown in 1940. Or the machine may be outdated because, as machinery makers keep warning, competitors may have installed more efficient, lower-cost machines. Or the customers may have moved, or the nearby raw materials been used up. The best-designed and best-located plant is built for a particular combination of raw materials, transport costs, and customers. If and when the circumstances change, the plant may have no more value than a prima donna's pitch in an empty theatre.

HORSE-AND-BUGGY FINANCE

Businessmen in the nineteenth century were unfamiliar with obsolescence. They only vaguely realized that the capital values they could build up in their generation could be wiped out in the next. Nor did they get any help from the economists. These men too had the hopeful notion that when a "capitalist" invested $100,000 in brick and stone, he had $100,000 of durable value, from which he could reasonably hope for a "reward," or profit, indefinitely, of so and so much per cent.

In fact the classical economists tended to see the capitalist as a sort of economic Flash Gordon, or Superman, who took plenty of risks, but always came out with a profit. (The Socialists, who didn't like the capitalist, accepted this picture—but with one change. They took off the wings and put on horns. This made him look like the Devil.)

One big reason why businessmen and economists used to overlook the importance of obsolescence was the business cycle. For ten or twenty years nearly everybody seemed to be making money. Then

29

would come a depression and panic, as in 1837, 1857, 1873, 1893. All the firms that were obsolete but didn't know it would go broke. But the cause seemed to be the panics.

CAUTION INCORPORATED

Modern business corporations can hardly be understood at all except against this background.

Limited Liability. To begin with, the modern corporation has "limited liability." This is the most important grant in its charter of incorporation. In fact English companies, in their titles, use the word "Limited" or "Ltd." instead of "Incorporated." The words mean the same. They do not mean that the firm is limited in its operations, but that the shareholders' liabilities are limited to the amount they have invested in the company. If the company fails, the stockholders cannot be sued individually for its debts, as members of a partnership can be.

This limitation became necessary when corporations became larger than private fortunes, and it made it possible for companies to offer their shares to strangers. The limited liability protected would-be shareholders against the financial perils mentioned above—chiefly of obsolescence.

CASH RESERVES

John D. Rockefeller is generally credited with being the first to build up the next corporate protection against obsolescence and the business cycle. The original Standard Oil Company was a refining company. Oil refiners were chronically being mowed down by insufficient cash. Rockefeller began building up cash reserves in good times in what seemed to most refiners quite unnecessary amounts. But as a result Standard survived panics and depressions. The reserves were largely built up by the plowing back into the business of profits that otherwise would have been paid out in dividends.

OTHER FINANCIAL PRECAUTIONS

Compared to nineteenth-century firms, modern corporations generally keep on hand far more "working capital" in proportion to their business. Working capital consists of the excess of cash, inventories, and accounts receivable, over debts that will come due soon.

Modern corporations also maintain more conservative "debt ratios." If a company has a net operating income of $1,000,000, and owes only $200,000 of interest on its bonds, its debt ratio is 5:1. If the million can be reasonably counted on each year, the ratio is conservative. But if the $1,000,000 of earnings this year may be followed by $1,000,000 loss next year, the ratio is not conservative; for two or three bad years could slay such a company financially. Bond-holders *have* to be paid *interest,* but stockholders don't have to be paid *dividends.*

The purpose of such policies is to protect the corporation against financial hazards. Essentially they are designed to enable it to outlast its existing machinery, products, and markets.

CONSERVATIVE ACCOUNTING

The same conservatism is also expressed in modern corporate accounting.

Most modern corporations periodically publish elaborate financial statements, in the form of a balance sheet and an earnings report. The purpose is to inform stockholders and creditors, *as fairly as possible,* of what the company has, and how it is doing—in terms of dollars.

These figures are meticulously checked. They are reviewed by independent auditors, who determine whether they "present fairly" the company's position and operations "in conformity with generally accepted accounting principles on a consistent basis." Then, if the company's shares are listed, the Stock Exchange also has a go at the figures, and so does the Securities and Exchange Commission in Washington.

Accounting has come a long way in this century. Compared to the primitive financial reports of earlier days, those of today are vastly more detailed—and vastly more conservative.

Some of the great corporate combinations of 1901 gave out no statements of income at all; and their balance sheets capitalized large amounts of promotional costs, resulting in what was even then called "watered stock." Today both profit-and-loss statements and published balance sheets are carefully itemized. More important, they show large deductions from property accounts for "depreciation." By this conservative policy, both earnings and property "book values" are kept down to more realistic levels.

DEPRECIATION VS. OBSOLESCENCE

Depreciation and obsolescence are two different things, and rarely do they come to the same amount.

OBSOLESCENCE

A depreciation charge is supposed to reflect the *wearing out* of a property. One way to figure it is to assume the property will last, say, 20 years; and so then to mark its value down each year by 5 per cent.

But at the end of 20 years, a property may with good luck still have considerable earning power. But it is more likely to be quite out of date. Many a single-purpose plant has been outmoded in five years. In fact, in fast-changing industries, plants are sometimes out of date by the time they are built.

It might be asked then, why a company doesn't change its books to make candid annual *obsolescence* charge-offs instead of depreciation write-downs of plant value.

Perhaps the best answer is that obsolescence is far too unpredictable to be reduced to any "generally accepted accounting principles." The best management in the world can only guess where obsolescence may come from next, and how soon.

For this reason alone, if for no other, the most conscientiously prepared financial statement falls short of telling the whole story of how a corporation is doing and is likely to do.

MANAGEMENT IN AN ERA OF PROGRESS AND OBSOLESCENCE

"The King was in his Counting House, Counting out his Money." So runs the old nursery rhyme. He seems to have been rich—in cash, at least. But his cash balance wouldn't show the state of his kingdom. Nor does a corporate cash balance show the company's prospects. Strong corporate reserves may combine with over-cautious policies to foreshadow a company's eventual downfall. Competitive business is still a matter of adventure in a changing world.

In the last analysis, corporate financial strength is only a means to an end. A strong balance sheet, showing ample working capital, is of value to a corporation chiefly as a means for managerial versatility in action.

With products and markets constantly changing, the management whose firms keep up are those that look most steadily ahead, and have the best answers to such questions as—"What new products can we make?" "How much capital can we risk in making them?" "How long will they sell?" and "What shall we make after that?"

OBSOLESCENCE

The author of "Alice in Wonderland" wrote:—

". . . in our country," said Alice, still panting a little, "you'd generally get to somewhere else—if you ran fast for a long time as we've been doing."

"A slow sort of country!" said the Red Queen. "Now here . . . it takes all the running you can do, to keep in the same place . . ."

It is usually said that companies are in business to make a profit; but in our lively American economy of today, it is equally true to say that they strive to make profits so as to stay in business.

An incidental result is that good business management is one important answer to the threat of technological unemployment. A strong and lasting corporation is about the nearest thing to job security that can be found in a progressive economy.

CHAPTER 5

"SHARING THE WEALTH"

THE PRINCIPLE OF SHARING

Ever since American free enterprise began pouring its new power into national circuits of economic energy, there has been talk of how we should *re*-distribute the wealth.

Yet no economic system has ever distributed its well-being more widely than ours. And this, mind you, is not *re*-distribution through taxes and welfare payments (which don't seem to accomplish their purpose very well anyway). It is a natural form of plain diffusion of wealth among all kinds of people.

In effect the producer must share with the buyer some of the benefits of the producer's special ability, in order to make his sales and so maintain his business. He does so either, as related in the section on Adventure, in an effort to make more profit by reaching for volume, or under the pressure of competition.

This is how "the man in the street" eventually gets to share the benefits of every growth industry, technological advance, and mass-production surge. This is not socialism. It is the essence of the free economy. It is plain *distribution,* or diffusion of wealth.

It works this way.

1. All business is done by agreements of some kind.
2. The agreements are voluntary.
3. Nobody agrees to anything unless he finds it in some way to his advantage.

A million deals, agreements, purchases, contracts and bargains are made every day in this country. They are all voluntary, and go on the same principle as that of the most primitive barter between Indians and fur-traders. Both sides gain, or think they gain.

This is the difference between ours and the Communist system—or any army system. (The Communists, in fact, seem to feel that a deal

34

is something like matching coins. One man's gain must be another man's loss.)

But because of this principle of sharing, or "letting the other fellow make a profit too," the free economy is one of history's greatest mechanisms for the diffusion of wealth.

WHAT PULLS UP WAGES

This principle of sharing applies to all markets, including the market for labor. The workman with labor to sell has been a consistent gainer from this sharing principle. This is because, though labor is a commodity, the price of which is subject to supply and demand, it is a unique commodity. It enters into every kind of production, and as productivity increases, the workman shares in the increase.

The hope of profit in new and growing industries forces employers in those industries to bid up for labor. This force has caused them to bid millions of people from off the farms, from out of depressed areas and out of domestic service, and even from across the Atlantic. The best and the most new jobs are normally found with the most optimistic employers who have the strongest hope of profit. And it is such labor markets that over the decades have steadily lifted wages.

The point where the workman repeatedly benefits from the sharing principle is in the wage-bargain. It is the peculiar nature of this bargain which benefits the workman. What the employer buys is *time*. But what he sells is *units of product* (or service). So as fast as he can get more units of product per hour of the time he buys, the time gets more valuable to him, and he can, and eventually will, one way or another, share the gains with the workman—even though the increased productivity may be due in large part to better machinery and management.

This is because if he doesn't, then even more successful or optimistic employers will outbid him in the labor market. His rate of "qualified applications" will go down, and his quit-rate will go up. If then he can't afford to "meet the (rising) market" for workmen's time, he is on the way to going out of business.

This is the "magic formula of productivity," which class-conscious European economists and employers failed to grasp. It is what Henry Ford meant when he said "There is no conflict, in a machine economy, between low costs and high wages." This is why the world's highest-paid labor (per hour of workman's time) can be and often is the

35

world's lowest-cost labor (per unit of output); whereas in some parts of Asia and Africa, labor is so expensive, in output or productivity, that it is the lowest-paid in the world, and in some cases scarcely worth any wage at all.

This is also why labor is a unique commodity, the market for which is normally quite different from that of all other commodities. The result of the productivity formula is that, in a free and progressive economy, and particularly in manufacturing industries, the price of an hour of labor normally and indefinitely tends to rise, while the price of manufactured goods normally and indefinitely tends to fall (or tends toward better goods for the same price).

But, it might be asked, "why doesn't the employing manufacturer's net return on sales also keep rising indefinitely?"

Obsolescence and competition are the combined reason. They are the two blades of the shears which keep clipping away the employer's gains. While the tide of increasing productivity continually works to

NEW PRODUCTS CREATE NEW OPPORTUNITIES
THE 747

increase the value of the workman's time, it continually pushes against the value of the employer's investment.

For example, he builds a new plant, with new machinery, to market a new product. It is a more productive plant, and he pays more for labor, accordingly. But in time a competitor, or a competing industry, builds a *still more productive* plant, and bids for people to man it. This notches up the labor market. But there is no such market for the outmoded plant. It is on the way to the scrap heap.

Perhaps this story might be criticized as skipping too easily over the problem of technological unemployment. It might be said that workmen can't move that fast, and labor is not that mobile. But they *can* move. Their time still has value. Outmoded plant can't move. It has no more than scrap value. There is no market today for steam locomotives except with the wreckers—nor any market for the shops that built these locomotives. But there is still a market for the time of the men who used to build and drive steam locomotives—though it may have taken them some time to find it.

THE "IRON LAW OF WAGES"

The forces that in a free economy normally tend to push up wages were wholly overlooked by most nineteenth-century economists. A century ago the still prevailing theory of wages, particularly in England, was called the "iron law of wages." The notion was that wages could not rise above what it took to keep the "working class" at a minimum of subsistence; the rest inevitably went to employers.

This unhappy theory of "capitalism" has long proved wrong in the free world, and it is mentioned here for only one reason. It was swallowed whole by the intellectual father of Communism, Karl Marx, and it is still, today, fixed Communist and Socialist dogma. Marx called what employers were supposed to naturally get, "a surplus value." He called this supposed "surplus value" the product of "the capitalist system of communal slave-holding."

Then, from this mistaken and bitter premise, he made what is probably the most mistaken economic forecast ever published. In 1848 he wrote angrily in the "Communist Manifesto":—

> *"Owing to the extensive use of machinery and to division of labor . . . the workman . . . becomes an appendage of the machine . . .*

37

"SHARING THE WEALTH"

"The lower strata of the middle class ... all sink gradually into the proletariat ...

"The modern laborer ... instead of rising with the progress of industry, sinks deeper and deeper below the conditions of existence of his own class. He becomes a pauper and pauperism develops more rapidly than population and wealth ..."

It is a colossal irony that today the only economic system in Europe that in any way resembles Marx' notion of "communal slave-holding" is that of Soviet Russia. If "pauper" means "one who takes what he gets and 'likes it,' " the Russian workman and farmer have been pauperized under an iron law of wages behind an iron curtain—the "surplus value" of their labor being expropriated by an iron government.

THE NATURAL BRAKES
ON WAGE IMPROVEMENT

While wages naturally keep advancing in a free economy, there are natural limits on the rate of advance. They cannot simply spurt ahead at the wish of wage-earners.

It is sometimes felt that they should advance with the general advance in national productivity. But this is far too broad a basis on which to justify particular wage advances in general; and it is proving hard to apply in specific cases. This is probably because national productivity does not increase "in general" but only by the particular advances of particular industries and firms. When we come down from the heights of overall national statistics, we see that ability to pay higher hourly wage rates varies sharply from industry to industry and from company to company.

Wage rates, like all other prices, are always competitive with something. The most immediate and visible competition to the price of an hour's labor is the cost of labor-saving machinery. The least visible competition is from other companies and industries.

Employers naturally check comparative costs on wages and on wage-saving machines. Hourly costs on machines are as easily figured as hourly direct-labor costs. And there can come a point, in the advance of hourly wage rates in a particular industry, where the employer, particularly under competitive pressure, may find it necessary to cut costs by "replacing labor with machinery." This point has been frequently reached in recent years in the automobile industry, where both automation and unemployment have been increasing side by side.

The competition less visible to the individual workman is that of other companies and, still further over the hill, of other industries. For instance, one reason why the steel industry in 1959 was so reluctant to raise wages, and why it did not then advance prices, was the growing threat of aluminum, plastics, and pre-stressed concrete.

If wages are pushed beyond their natural rate of growth, they will cause a change in employers' investments, in two ways—both meaning less jobs. Excessive wage increases will needle the employer to put his money into *more job-reducing* automation, and *less job-producing* expansion. As a result, high, non-seasonal, chronic unemployment in an industry may mean that its wage rates have been pushed too high, or above their "natural market." Such unemployment, or surplus of labor, is analogous to the surpluses of farm products which result from government support of crop prices above what consumers are willing to pay. The results may be fine for those who still have high-paying jobs, but not so good for those whose labor has been "priced out of the market."

PROFITS

The Bible says in three places "Thou shalt not muzzle the ox that treadeth out the corn." Moses said it once (Deuteronomy 25:4) and Paul said it twice (I Corinthians 9:9, and I Timothy 5:18). Both law-givers meant the same thing. The Biblical ox, like the modern employer, figured to pick up some grains of corn while treading out his job. This is a pretty good analogy for the modern corporation. It has to eat, too, but will sometimes work on gleanings.

Employers labor to proclaim the importance of profits. They call them the tonic, the sparkplug, and the energizer to our economic system, and the seed-corn for our future growth. I would rather say that the hope of profit is the pituitary gland that regulates growth in the economic body, or the electronic tube or transistor that multiplies effects. But every man to his own figures of speech.

In any case two things are certain. First, no hope of profit, no jobs. And second, the more the hope of profit, the more and better the jobs. What is left to the employer, in any wage contract, is money invested for the employee, in future job security. If this isn't so, the workman is in the wrong industry, or working under the wrong management.

"SHARING THE WEALTH"

The argument is fallacious that labor should get *all* the benefit of increasing productivity. This is the basic Marxian theory. Pushed with consistent success, it would mean, "no private employers."

One thing is fairly sure. If wages are negotiated too high, too soon, they will either (1) cause higher prices, in an inflation era, or (2) cause unemployment, in a stable-price or a deflationary era. Timing is of the essence. Even the fast-growing American economy can move ahead only so fast, and its gains must be shared.

COMMON INTERESTS

The workman and the employer have common interests. It seems obvious that the company, the employees, and the unions must work together. The more each contributes to the joint pie to be cut, the more each can hope to gain—just as the more a man contributes to his job, the more persuasively he can argue when he asks for a raise.

CHAPTER 6

OPPORTUNITY

By their fruits ye shall know them. The Founding Fathers of this republic set up a constitution to create a minimum of government, and so to protect the liberties of individuals.

And this nation responded with adventure, competition, economic progress, and a sharing of the gains which have given us the highest standard of living in the world.

We have had both liberty *and* progress—and still have them after 180 years.

Meantime, since World War II, something similar has been happening abroad. What could almost be called a *"prosperity* explosion" has occurred in other parts of the "Free World" among the "western-style democracies." In particular Japan and Germany, defeated in war, have thrown off their authoritarian ideas of government, turned to free enterprise instead, and made astounding economic recoveries. They have grown even faster in the last 25 years than we have. And the other democracies—France, Italy, Britain, and smaller western nations, have kept only slightly behind them in material progress.

This progress has been in direct proportion to the degree to which these countries have rejected strong centralized government, and turned toward individual initiative. Having done so, they have rapidly increased both their industrial and their farm production.

THE BIGGEST BACKWARD COUNTRY

Now let us consider a great country that exemplifies the negative of free enterprise—Russia—and consider how its people are faring.

Ever since the 1917 revolution the Communists have been telling the Russian people that they would soon outstrip the western world in prosperity. And after the Russians astonished the world by launching Sputnik—the first space vehicle—in 1957, they began boasting to the United States that they would soon outdo us in material well-being. Premier Khrushchev on his visit here repeated this boast many times. And many people in this country took it seriously.

41

OPPORTUNITY

Surely no one does now. The deadweight effect of Communist controls on the Russian economy has become all too obvious in the 1960's—on Russian farming, Russian industry, and Russian living standards. Russia is lagging as the most backward among the large countries of Europe.

The best evidence of this is in Russian farming. Before the revolution, Russia was a great agricultural country. Southern Russia—the Ukraine—was sometimes called the "breadbasket" of Europe, to which it exported grains in exchange for manufactured goods. But this is no longer so. The per-acre yield of all grains in Russia is about a third of the U.S. yield. And in the 1960's Russia had to *import* over 600 million bushels of wheat from the free world.

The Soviets explain this on the ground that they have put their official emphasis on industrialization. But here, except for expansion in steel and in electric power, the record is just about as dismal.

There are not many more than a million vehicles on the poor highways of Russia, and most of them are in the hands of government officials and Communist party members. The figure for the U.S.A. is 100 million. About 8 million new cars are turned out yearly in this country.

(And if Russian citizens had even a tenth, instead of a hundredth, as many cars as we have, they would have rough riding indeed. The Soviets have built hardly any modern roads in the last 50 years, and filling stations—not "service stations"—are few and far between.)

The Russians, though skilled at handicraft, don't seem able, under Communism, to master the arts of mass production. After having produced a few hundred thousand copies of older American models, in the 1960's they got the Italian Fiat company to come in and build a Russian plant to make 400,000 cars a year—a twentieth of American annual production. And while the Soviets have greatly increased their basic steel production, they cannot seem to master the complex mass chemical processes of producing the new plastics whose production has been multiplying since World War II in the U.S.A.

For another evidence, take Russian housing. Except for the homes of officials and party members, it is the worst in Europe. In the late 1960's the Soviets *planned* to increase living quarters to where everyone could have 100 square feet per person—not much more than the average prison cell in this country. This, however, is a maximum; no one may legally have more. It amounts to a single room 20 feet square for four persons! Few Russians have running water in their homes—city or country. Fewer still have telephones. Some cities don't even have telephone directories.

By and large the Russian people still live not much better than they did before the revolution—and that was about as well as Americans lived in, say, 1900 or before.

DEADWEIGHT CONTROLS

The reasons for this lie at the heart of the Soviet system. It is skilfully devoted to concentrating power in the hands of the Central Committee of the Communist Party. But that means an inevitable overcentralization of everything, and a consequent suppression of individual initiative. Everything is planned from the top down. Orders go down from Moscow to the collective farms on how much to plant, and when, and when to harvest; and to the individual plant managers, how much to produce, and where to get the raw materials. The Russians have no marketing system as we know it.

In consequence, there is, in their industry and farming, neither adventure, nor competition, nor natural progress. No one has any incentive to break out of this upside-down system—in fact the individual faces severe punishment if he does. What "the Party" says, goes —or else.

Nor is Russia the only great country where normal economic life is being stunted. It goes on also in China. That intermittently halfstarved country also, in recent years, has had to buy millions of tons of grain from the Free World to keep its people alive, yet its industry remains infantile, except in the field of rocketry.

In fact it may be said in general that the more a nation's economy is centrally controlled, the more its economic troubles. And, conversely, a nation's economic progress is directly determined by the extent to which individuals are free to organize businesses, manage them according to their own lights, and sell the products into a free, competitive market.

MODERN FEUDALISM

All this, however, is only the *material* side of the story. Unfortunately for the Russian people, the same heavy hand that holds down the nation's economic initiative, also enforces conformity in politics,

OPPORTUNITY

arts and letters. The Russian dissenter has to keep his mouth shut on all political matters, or informers in his village, or city block, will get him in trouble. Russians have no freedom of speech and no free press. Like medieval serfs, they cannot travel from one part of Russia to another (let alone leave the country) without police permission. Books, even of fiction, that deviate from the Communist "party line," can be published only by being smuggled out to the free world. The human spirit is shackled whether it is devoted to material things or to cultural pursuits. To keep themselves in power the Communists must suppress individual initiative no matter *what* form it takes.

But this does not mean that the Soviet system is no threat to us. The fact that their power system stultifies Russian material and spiritual growth doesn't prevent them from concentrating on great ballistic missiles, navies and armies. The Communists have a huge disposable income or surplus value taken out of the hides of 200,000,000 Russians and their satellites. With these resources they are as large and constant a threat to us as were the Indians to our frontier forefathers. The more we gain on them economically, the more they will covet our prosperity.

In the last two centuries autocratic Russian governments have been a threat successively to the Swedes, the Germans, the Bulgarians, the Roumanians, the Greeks, the Turks, the British, the French, the Finns, and the central-European Slavs. We inherit these threats. We have to out-match the Communists in war-power, no matter what the cost.

HOW GOVERNMENTS SPREAD

The Communist idea of government is the exact converse of that of the Founding Fathers of the United States. While ours was a *minimum* of government, theirs has turned out to be a *maximum* of government. (And theirs also has become a "Novus Ordo Seclorum," though the opposite of ours. No such meticulous absolutism has ever been known before in human history.)

All governments, as our forefathers feared, tend this way, if not held in check by right principles, such as underlie the Constitution. Governments, by the nature of men, are like coiled springs, which expand unless kept in check.

Their reach for power is a natural thing—though in the wrong place. Just as people in the business world reach for profits by offering better goods and services, so legislators and government officials reach

44

for power by promising things to some of us at the expense of the rest of us.

These ambitions are encouraged by some writers, who try to top the American economic achievement by encouraging a "revolution of rising expectations." No matter how fast things improve, the critics chorus "Faster!" And no matter what the new expectations call for, it is now the federal government that is supposed to fulfill them.

These extensions of government power are usually sought in the name of "the general welfare," or, in today's term, "the public interest." But it seldom works that way. The drive for more government action is usually successful only when it is backed by special interests, seeking to obstruct or burden some form of economic adventure or competition that may disturb such special interests.

This is what happened before our Revolution. The colonies objected to a mesh of obstructions, enforced by the Crown, blocking their economic growth. These obstructions were supposed to be in the national interest of all Britain; but, as Adam Smith pointed out in his "Wealth of Nations," they were actually in the private interest of certain companies of British merchants.

To the argument, in short, that we "need a strong government," the answer is that we need most of all a strong *nation*—and, serving that strong nation, a government strong only in national defense and the maintenance of "domestic tranquility." Big government is essentially the deadening and wasteful business of minding other people's business. "That government is best, which governs least."

OPPORTUNITY AND FUTURE

A generation from now, if we keep our government under bounds, it seems safe to guess that American living will have changed in ways we can hardly now imagine. The natural ingenuity of man will have made generally available, means of working and playing as inconceivable today as the steam engine would have been to George Washington or the telephone to Abraham Lincoln.

It is customary now to predict an almost steadily rising standard of living for the rest of this century. But this is to look toward only one aspect of the picture. The other aspect is the opportunity this will give the coming generation for the exercise of the creative spirit. For higher living standards are only one feature of our American way of life.

OPPORTUNITY

Equally important is a continuous series of challenges to significant individual achievement.

And to these we can reasonably look forward. There is no sign that the supply of opportunities will run out. Ours is a society in which change is a constant element. There will be, for instance, growth industries not yet even born, of which modern electronics, chemistry, and space technology are only forerunners. And the dreams of today will be the jobs of tomorrow.

In such a world, the creative spirit of man should continue to find outlet. Man's innate tendency to dream, to innovate and to excel, should find continued satisfaction in achievements.

MAN REACHES THE MOON

Nor does this necessarily mean spectacular achievements. The creative spirit is not expressed solely in painting, sculpture or music; nor in acting as pastor, priest or rabbi to a flock; nor in writing best sellers, influential editorials, or poetry. The business of the world takes adventure, competition and new ideas in such down-to-earth callings as those of farmer, carpenter, truck driver, salesman, repair man, or computer programmer. It takes everybody to know everything about the busy world in which we serve each other. It should remain a world of opportunities.